a celebration of

Norfolk Punts

1926 - 2006

Jamie Campbell (signature)

by
Jamie Campbell

First published in this edition in 2006 for the Norfolk Punt Class

by

Hamilton Publications Ltd.,
9 Marine Parade,
Gorleston on sea,
Norfolk. NR 31 6DU.

www.hamiltonpublications.com

ISBN 0 903094 17 7

Printed in Great Britain by Total Paper Management Ltd.,
57 - 61 Pitt Street, Norwich, Norfolk. NR3 1DE.

Cover photographs by Anna Gill.

Front: Traditional, Morrison and Wyche & Coppock designs racing together. Mike Evans, crewed by Donald Forbes in *Swallow II*, Mike Morrison in *Cormorant* and David Houghton in *Firefly*.

Rear: Norfolk Punts tied up on the Norfolk Punt Club pontoons in 1999.

BLAKENEY

SHERINGHAM

CROMER

FAKENHAM

NORTH WALSHAM

AYLSHAM

STALHAM

OXNEAD

Barton
Broad

Hickling
Broad

POTTER
HEIGHAM

ELMHAM

R.Bure

R. Ant

R. Wensum

Ormesby
Broad

WROXHAM

R. Thurne

Filby
Broad

Ranworth
Broad

R. Tud

R.Bure

ACLE

GT.
YARMOUTH

NORWICH

R. Yare

REEDHAM

Fritton
Decoy

R. Yare

R. Chet

LODDON

LOWESTOFT

HAMILTON'S
NAVIGATIONS

R. Waveney

BECCLES

OULTON
BROAD

BUNGAY

A watercolour of 'Scientific' Fuller, painted in his punt at Rockland by Frank Southgate in about 1900.

A watercolour by Arthur Batchelor dated 1924, showing a punt being 'shoved'. The caption is AB to HL. A note on the rear of the painting reads "to Her Ladyship, in spite of having her hair bobbed." HL was Auriol Wingard.

This painting has been reproduced by kind permission of Arthur Batchelor's granddaughter, Mrs. Karen Curtis.

A watercolour of the Norfolk Punt Club pontoons at Barton, painted for the Author by Adrian Taunton (Punt 38 *Sandpiper*) in 1994 and reproduced with his kind permission.

This painting of *Swallow II* and *Decoy* was presented to J.M.Evans on his retirement as Executive Director of the International Yacht Racing Union in Hamburg in November 1995. This is another painting by Adrian Taunton and has again been reproduced with his kind permission. The rear of the painting is signed by the entire IYRU Council, including HM King Constantine of Greece and HM King Harald of Norway.

Chapter One
Roots

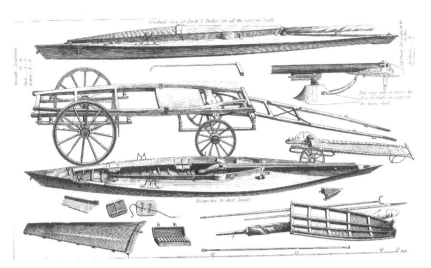

"Punt and equipment for a 200lb gun."

Instructions to Young Sportsmen by Lt. Col. Peter Hawker, first published in 1833

Walter White wrote in 1866 that hovels occupied by agricultural workers near Potter Heigham were at least as bad as any he'd seen in Ireland but from their overcrowded towns and cities, the Victorians managed to overlook the most abject poverty and viewed the Broads as a rural idyll. Broads dwellers did enjoy a certain freedom; game was protected but fish and fowl were free. Punts were the usual craft employed for wildfowling and fishing. Punt gunning is a stalking art and the craft were painted matt grey, "the colour of a kittiwake's back" to provide minimum notice of their approach. The punt would often be hand-paddled to the quarry, with the gunner lying prone in the bottom. When a shot presents itself, the gunner bangs his hand on the side of the punt and fires as the duck take to wing. Those fowl not killed outright by

P.H.Emerson used a full plate (24") camera in 1886 and exposed three separate plates for each photograph, as early chemicals provided insufficient range of exposure. The photograph is inevitably posed but shows just how a gunner might approach fowl.

WildLife and Landscape. pub. 1886

the big gun were trimmed up with a shoulder gun carried on board and rather unfortunately known as a 'cripple-stopper.' Punt gunning gets bad press today as something approaching a weapon of mass destruction but the the old guns have a range limited to about sixty yards. Later, breech loaders and more sophisticated, double barrelled four bore shot guns were mounted on punts but the early muzzle loaders were limited to a single shot per outing. Stalking packs of wary, wild duck in mid-winter requires great skill and patience. Large numbers of fowl to a single shot usually owe more to the tap room than the estuary. It has always been illegal to go in direct pursuit of fowl using any kind of artificial power and rather than rowing long distances, the gunners began to set 'leg o'mutton' sails. Their punts, without keel or lee boards and steered with an oar off the quarter, began, under some conditions to sail surprisingly quickly.

right
Sir Ralph Payne-Galway's recommended rig for a gun punt, first published in 1882.

A Fowler in Ireland.

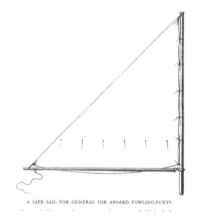

A SAFE SAIL FOR GENERAL USE ABOARD FOWLING-PUNTS.

Mr. Richard Fielding Harmer in punt-gunning costume.
Broadland Sport 1902

far right
Two photographs of Arthur Patterson in his punt *Yarwhelp*, taken for his book *Through Broadland in a Breydon Punt*. pub. 1920.

Breydon Water is the spiritual home of Broads punt gunning. Many of the old time Breydon gunners; 'Short'un' Page and 'Pintail' Thomas were made famous by Great Yarmouth naturalist Arthur Patterson, who wrote for the Eastern Daily Press under the pseudonym 'John Knowlittle'. In the market gunners heyday, Breydon Water was brackish, not saline as it is today and much of the bank was lined with reed and weed that provided ideal habitat for their quarry.

Their punts were typically double-ended; long and low in the water, flat bottomed and slab sided - easy and cheap to build. Overall length would vary according to the weight of the gun - a nine or ten foot gun might weigh 180lbs. The Breydon market gunners were often joined by 'gentleman gunners', shooting for pleasure and it wasn't long before gun punts began to set lugsails and eventually copied the gunter sloop rigs that Frank Morgan Giles developed for his sophisticated fourteen foot, West of England Conference dinghies. Structural alterations designed to increase scour and save Great Yarmouth Port & Haven Commissioners' dredging costs caused the Breydon mudflats to pile up and increased salt incursion. Patterson always maintained that Breydon was the price paid for Yarmouth harbour.

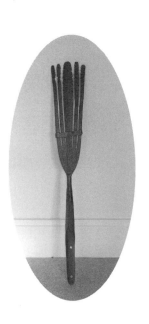

left

Essential equipment for punts. Left to right: ligger and bait (for pike) stick and eel bab (worms threaded on wool) eel dart, eel pick, weed rake, pole and quant.

photo: Life and Sport on the Norfolk Broads. Oliver G. Ready. pub.1910

far left
close up of an eel pick.

Photographed by courtesy of John Mauger

left

Bob Parker of Rockland photographed in 1914 with his punt gun over his shoulder and his "cripplestopper" in his right hand. He died in 1930 at the age of 101. Once a wherryman, he used to fish and shoot Rockland Broad, selling his ducks "to the gentry in the Close."

photo: Robert Malster

The punts used at Hickling enjoyed a much gentler environment than their Breydon sisters and began to evolve quite separately. Calmer waters enabled a larger, more open cockpit. Quanting was easier than rowing around the shallow, tideless waters and reed beds and to support a man standing upright, the Hickling punts developed a wider floor at the rear of their cockpit. By around 1910, hard chines had begun to evolve into the pleasing curves seen on local reed lighters. They developed a little shape to their keel and bow and sterns became gently rounded for ease of manoeuvring. Hulls began to be built with clinker topsides and carvel bottoms. The Hickling punts of yore were the direct antecedent of the traditional Norfolk Punt.

Lord Desborough's punt
Pochard, **outside**
Whiteslea Lodge, near
Hickling Broad.

photo: unknown

Lord Desborough KG,
GCVO

Lord Desborough and his famous 'keeper Jim Vincent were past masters of the art of 'shoving' a punt. Gerald Sambrooke Sturgess recalled: "His Lordship was a familiar sight on a summers day, dressed in white flannels, a Leander club blazer and a straw hat with the club's hatband, standing erect in the stern of his punt; 'shoving' her with a beautifully easy, slow and rhythmical but deceptively powerful action. She moved through the water with scarcely a ripple, smoothly, swiftly, noiselessly and apparently effortlessly, in a way that no modern punt could ever hope to emulate!"

Lord Desborough and Jim Vincent both died in 1944.

Jim Vincent shows his sister Ida Grosvenor, a double barrelled, four bore punt gun.

Mrs. Grosvenor shot for Great Britain at the 1936 Olympic Games in Berlin.

photo: Grosvenor

left

Blue Quill on the Thurne in about 1922.

photo: NPC Handbook

far left

Prawn.

photo: Stewart Morris Collection

A thirteen year old Stewart Morris won the first Norfolk Punt race ever recorded, at Hickling regatta in August 1923 sailing his father's old punt *Prawn*, built in 1908. The Morris family hailed from Reigate Heath in Surrey but spent most of their summers on board their wherry *Sundog* at Broads regattas. Father, Harold Morris owned a number of boats, including the punts *Shrimp* and *Prawn*, several fourteen foot dinghies and from 1919, the Yare & Bure *Bath White*. Younger son Stewart had been taught to sail by a Hickling man from a large and well known local family. Cubit Nudd was employed as the Morris family skipper and had earlier taught the well-known naturalist and photographer Emma Turner to sail on Hickling Broad. Later in his life he was employed as a sailmaker at Herbert Woods boatyard at Potter Heigham.

Cubit Nudd

photo: Broadland Birds, E.L.Turner. pub. 1924

Walter Woods builders plate in *Shrimp*.

photo: Mike Evans

A.T.Chittock with his daughter Betty in 1923.

photo: Judy Macdonald (nee Sturgess) and Peter Sturgess

The following year, Hickling Open Regatta offered the Wortley Rose Bowl for a punt race. A group of sailors from Brundall fancied their chances for the new trophy and took their punts around to Hickling for the event. The 'Brundall Boys' punts were often amateur built and usually encouraged by George Marshall. Jim Vincent fitted out Lord Desborough's *Pochard* and Harold Morris won the event with William Jermy second with *Venture*. Gerald Sambrooke Sturgess reported that the "Brundall punts were well beaten" but W.F.Jermy in a letter to Dr. Tracey in 1960 had an entirely different recollection; claiming that he had taken first place in *Venture*, with *Prawn* second, Jack Edge third in *Hetebe* and brother Jermy in fourth place, "the rest of the Hickling punts were not in it." The trophy wasn't engraved for several years so we'll probably never know the true story but the differing perspectives provide an interesting basis for a thriving class.

In 1925, *Prawn* again beat two Brundall boats. The following year, Jim Vincent borrowed a large rig from the half-decker *Never Mind* and carried off the Wortley Rose Bowl in *Pochard*. At about the same time a young boatbuilder who had been apprenticed to his father at Potter Heigham also took *Pochard* for a sail. She was a punt that his uncle had built. Almost unnoticed, the foundations of the Norfolk Punt class were beginning to fall into place.

Arthur Batchelor taking Pull's Ferry across the Wensum.

photo: courtesy Mrs. Karen Curtis

Arthur Batchelor lived in Albermarle Road, Norwich and was a privileged young man, able to indulge his wide ranging artistic temperament. He was a talented painter and collected folksongs with his friend Vaughan Williams. Batchelor was also a skilled angler and one of a group of friends (including Russell Colman) who were invited to fish with Tod Corbett at his fishing 'hut' at Evanger in Norway. Tod and his brother Frank Corbett were both keen sportsmen. They founded the Broads One Design class in 1901 and found time whilst in Norway to teach the locals cricket.

Chapter 2
The Norfolk Punt Club

In August 1926, Arthur Bachelor of Albermarle Road, Norwich started some lively correspondence in the Eastern Daily Press about Norfolk Punts. It quickly became apparent that interest was widespread and a meeting was held at the Bridewell in Norwich on Saturday 11th December 1926. Present were: Arthur Bachelor, W.Britton, A.T.Chittock, H.W.Crotch, J.ff Edge, C.R.Howlett, W.F.Jermy, H.J.Starling and Herbert Woods. They decided to form The Norfolk Punt Club. The objective of their new club was "to preserve and if possible, improve the traditional local type of punt and to encourage competitions in quanting, rowing and sailing of same." Arthur Bachelor was asked to write to the Eastern Daily Press giving notice of a further meeting to be held the following Saturday, 18th December 1926, to discuss the necessary constitutional details. At this meeting, Harold Morris was elected the first commodore; Arthur Bachelor vice commodore and Herbert Woods took the junior flag rank. Jack ffiske Edge of Holm Close, Brundall became the club's first honourary secretary and treasurer. (His son, Pat Edge later raced an Ajax at Lowestoft) The first club year (1927) book lists seventeen members.

Arthur Bachelor
- a self portrait.

courtesy: Hugh Wylam

The club lost no time in measuring existing Norfolk Punts and formulating class rules for new boats. Overall length was permitted to vary between sixteen feet and twenty two feet; and in common with the National Fourteen foot dinghy class, spars had to stow within the hull. This restriction virtually imposed a gunter sloop rig, although some early boats persisted with a balanced lug. Sail area was restricted to eight square feet, per foot of overall length. The maximum cost of the hull was fixed at £2 per foot of overall length and the cost of all other gear could not exceed £15: 15s: 0d. The cost of a twenty two foot punt was effectively limited to £60. A handicap system was agreed of ten seconds per foot of overall length.

Harold Morris
Commodore
1926 - 1930

photo: Stewart Morris
collection

10

NORFOLK PUNT CLUB.

DEFINITIONS AND REGULATIONS.

1. That a Norfolk Punt be defined as a strongly-built light draught, open or partly decked wooden craft, with very low free-board and nearly flat bottom, suited to the purpose of being quanted, rowed, or sailed to fowl.

2. LENGTH—Maximum 22 ft., minimum 16 ft.
   BEAM from 4 to 5½, beams to her length.
   VERTICAL EXTREME of hull without coaming, 18 ins.
   VERTICAL EXTREME of coaming 4 ins., and no fittings to show above coaming.
   SPRING OF FLOOR measured inside stem and stern pieces, maximum 3 ins.
   ATHWARTSHIP ROUND OF FLOOR, maximum 2 ins.
   AREA OF OPEN WELL at least equal to decked-in portion.

11

MINIMUM WIDTH OF OPEN WELL three-quarters of extreme beam.
MAXIMUM FIXED DRAUGHT, 1 foot.
MINIMUM PLANKING — Bottom ⅜ in., sides ⅜ in., deck ⅛ in.
Carvel-built Punts are excluded.

3. Leeboards, centre-plates, or keels must be easily removable, their exposed area must not exceed 4 square feet, nor their weight 50 lbs. Rudder must be removable.

4. All spars must stow inside the boat, and no chain, plates, seat, or other excrescence shall project beyond the planking.

5. No shifting ballast.

6. Crews not to exceed 3, nor sail area 8 square feet to a foot.

7. Except as regards 3 and 6 these regulations shall not apply to craft existing on 31st December, 1926.

The first set of class rules, published in the 1927 club hand book.

courtesy: Robert Malster

The new club lost no time in building new punts and Horace Bolingbroke commissioned *Scud* from William Mollett of Bishopgate in Norwich. She was finished in February 1927 and cost a princely £27: 0s: 0d.

32 Bishopgate St.
~~WELL'S FERRY.~~
NORWICH, *Feb 3rd 1927*

H. Bolingbroke Esq

Dr. to W. E. MOLLETT,
BOAT BUILDER.

REPAIRS OF EVERY DESCRIPTION.

BOATS HOUSED. & MOTOR LAUNCHES AND BOATS FOR HIRE.

To Building 18' x 4'.3" Gun Punt
Materials
Bottom Planking 5/8 Red Wood
Side " 3/8 Wht Wood
Decks & stem 1/2 Red "
Stem & Stern Post Oak
Timbers Beams Coaming Oak
Galvd Nails to Timbers
Copper Nails & Roves for Planking
Brass Screws
Centre Plate & Rudder Iron Galvd
Pole Mast Bamboo Spars
Cotton Sheet Manilla Halyards
Straight Paddle Ashoe Fir
Galvd Rowlocks
Union Sail by Ladies 2 Reefings
3 Coats Paint Color as desired
or Painted & Varnished ..

Estimate Not to Exceed £27

Received on Afc Twenty Pounds 10
Feb 32nd 1
W. E. Mollett

**Horace and Ciceley
Bolingbroke sailing** *Scud.*

photo: Robert Malster

In the summer of 1928, *Scud* was taken on a Broads adventure. First she travelled along the North Walsham & Dilham Canal.

North Walsham & Dilham Canal.

***Scud* at Dee bridge between Honing and Dilham.**

photo: Robert Malster

North Walsham & Dilham Canal.

***Scud* above Austin Bridge 21.6.28.**

photo: Robert Malster

They were able to reach just above Swafield. Robert Malster recalls Horace telling him that the trip was hard work and the photograph album of the voyage records broken down locks even in those days. *Scud* was a heavy old boat and had to be carried across unusable locks and weirs. Unsatisfied with the North Walsham & Dilham Canal, Horace and an unidentified crew set off to see how far they could reach along the upper Bure.

***Scud* was towed to the Rising Sun, Coltishall behind Horace Bolingbroke's motorcycle. 14.7.28.**

photo: Robert Malster

Aylsham had once been accessible to wherries and the pair reached Burgh next Aylsham. A rig that fitted inside the hull must have been a great advantage for portage and camping on board.

Scud at Cradle Bridge, Burgh next Aylsham.

photo: Robert Malster

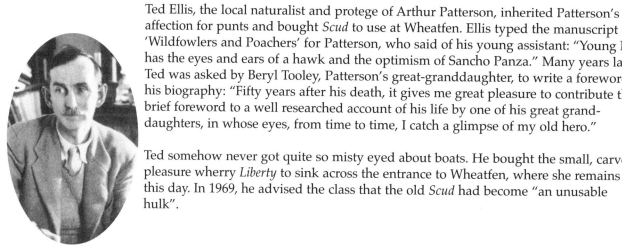

Ted Ellis, the local naturalist and protege of Arthur Patterson, inherited Patterson's affection for punts and bought *Scud* to use at Wheatfen. Ellis typed the manuscript of 'Wildfowlers and Poachers' for Patterson, who said of his young assistant: "Young Ellis has the eyes and ears of a hawk and the optimism of Sancho Panza." Many years later, Ted was asked by Beryl Tooley, Patterson's great-granddaughter, to write a foreword to his biography: "Fifty years after his death, it gives me great pleasure to contribute this brief foreword to a well researched account of his life by one of his great grand-daughters, in whose eyes, from time to time, I catch a glimpse of my old hero."

Ted somehow never got quite so misty eyed about boats. He bought the small, carvel pleasure wherry *Liberty* to sink across the entrance to Wheatfen, where she remains to this day. In 1969, he advised the class that the old *Scud* had become "an unusable hulk".

Ted Ellis

photo: Eastern Daily Press

With over seven hundred members in the 1890s, the Yare Sailing Club had claimed to be the largest sailing club in the world but propelled by improved personal transport and the new sugar beet factory at Cantley, Broads yachting began to migrate steadily to the North Rivers. By 1924, Horning Town S.C. had become the largest club boasting over four hundred members. Yacht racing on the Broads between the wars was very different from the territorial affairs we know today. The Royal Norfolk & Suffolk Yacht Club was alone in enjoying their own premises; despite only rarely racing from Lowestoft.

THURSDAY, JULY 19th,

Norfolk Punt Club Regatta.

Start 10-30 a.m.

Sailed under the Rules of the Norfolk and Suffolk Regatta Association.

Race 1. NORFOLK BROADS & YARE AND BURE O.D.C. Sweepstakes
  Entry Fee 5/-

Race 2. NORFOLK GUN PUNTS. Classes A and B.

Rule 3. 14 ft. NATIONAL DINGHIES. Sweepstakes.
  Entry Fee 5/-

Race 4. NORFOLK GUN PUNTS, Classes A and B. (Invitation Race.)

Race 5. HALF-DECKED RESTRICTED CLASS & Gt. YARMOUTH ONE
    DESIGN CLASS SAILS. Sweepstakes.   Entry Fee 5/-

Rule 6. NORFOLK GUN PUNTS, Classes A and B. (Ladies to steer.)
    O. R. HOWLETT, Hon. Sec.

Hunting, Printer, St. Miles, Norwich.

By 1928, the Norfolk Punt Club were pleased to be invited to organise a day at Wroxham Regatta.

Most local clubs ran their regattas at a wide variety of Broads locations and often on consecutive days. Yachtsmen usually belonged to several clubs and it was not uncommon to find individuals serving as officers of two simultaneously. In 1932, Byron V. Noel was commodore of both the Norfolk Punt Club and Horning Town Sailing Club. Racing, whilst keen, was carried out in a gentlemanly manner amongst friends. The secretary of the Great Yarmouth Yacht Club in 1932 was A.T.Chittock and nineteen Norfolk Punts were owned by their members. A typical programme might include cruiser races, split into two starts (large and small), White boats, Brown boats and Yarmouth one designs, Norfolk Punts, International and Norfolk fourteen foot dinghies and an open & half decked class. Turnouts for individual races were not high and only three or four entries not uncommon. The casual observer might have to look at the burgee flying over the Yare & Bure S.C.houseboat to work out which club was running the racing on a particular day.

far left
Y&BSC Houseboat at Wroxham Broad.

photo: Norfolk Broads Yacht Club

left
The Y&BSC houseboat on its way to Beccles.

photo: Ken. Clabburn

Lunch on board the Y&BSC houseboat. l to r. Sir E.J. (Jack) Mann, Mrs. W.L.Clabburn and Byron V. Noel - N.P.C. commodore from 1930 - 1936.

photo: Ken.Clabburn

The Yare and Bure Sailing Club houseboat was towed to regattas with a launch strapped alongside (with some difficulty) by their steward, William Yardley and used by most clubs to run their racing. Other clubs were charged six guineas a day for use of the facility. Yardley served drinks, cold lunches and teas aboard, fired the guns and broke out and lowered the race flags; whilst the race committee ran their races from the roof of the houseboat. On regatta days a gun was fired at 0800 for vessels to make colours and another at sunset to strike them. All of the larger boats attending regattas would have paid hands on board and this ceremony was punctiliously observed - a nice piece of flag etiquette that seems to have largely disappeared.

Charles Carrodus was Eastern Daily Press, Yachting Correspondent for thirty years and a Yachting Monthly columnist. He was elected an honourary member of the Norfolk Punt Club in 1933.

photo: Horace Grant

Charles Carrodus noted one July that there was not a day without a regatta until September 5th. The fleet started out in early July at Wroxham with three consecutive days organised by the Royal Norfolk & Suffolk Y.C., the Great Yarmouth Y.C. and the Yare & Bure S.C., followed by three days at Thurne Mouth run by the Y.&B.S.C. and Horning Town Sailing Club. The circuit progressed to Acle for two days organised by the Y.&B.S.C. and Gt.Y.Y.C., finishing with a passage race to Horning on Wednesday. Thursday and Friday were Wroxham Open regatta and from 1932, the punts raced from Wood's Dyke in Horning to Brown's Hill on the Ant on their way back for Barton Open Regatta on August Bank Holiday Monday. (then in early August). Tea was provided on the lawn at Brown's Hill, a house that Byron V. Noel built at Ludham. Noel was one of Lord Byron's Christian names. The couple died without issue, so the family should not be upset to hear Mrs. Noel described as "fat, plain and Scots" by a distant relation! The following Tuesday, the punts raced from Potter Heigham to Hickling for the Open regatta on Wednesday. Thursday was traditionally Potter Heigham regatta. On Friday, the Punt class held their own regatta at Hickling and the rest of the fleet moved down to the south rivers for Beccles, Oulton and Lowestoft Sea Week.

Following the racing fleet was a flotilla of larger yachts, wherries and houseboats that accommodated their owners and friends for the summer in some style. Most had a paid hand or two to look after the boats and cook. Many kept good cellars and an invitation to dinner on board ensured a good evening. Races for Norfolk Punts were quickly included in most regattas on the North rivers as the new club was quickly absorbed into the circuit. The class was a mixture of the well-to-do and the not so well-off, who often built their own punts. The Morris family had the counter sterned, motor wherry *Sundog*, A.T.Chittock *Caister Maid*, a converted Yarmouth beach yawl and the Fitt family owned a large motor cruiser called *Dawn*. As each regatta finished, the fleet moved to the next venue.

Y&BSC regatta. Acle. Monday July29th 1930.

Prawn **gets the best of a start at Acle. Stewart Morris is crewed by Peter Scott.**

photo: Stewart Morris

far left Horning Town Regatta.

photo: Desmond Truman collection

left *Trout* **owned by Eric Morris (brother of Harold) at Horning regatta. September 1928.**

photo: Ken. Clabburn

Betty Chittock, crewed by 'Young' Walter Woods for the Ladies race at Horning regatta in 1929.

photo: Judy Macdonald (nee Sturgess) and Peter Sturgess

In 1929, Herbert Woods designed and built his first punt, the twenty foot *Flight*. Gerald Sambrooke Sturgess later described Woods as "an experienced helm, a good designer and a clever salesman." His punts made their debut on the first day of Wroxham Week and each one marked a significant improvement in performance over the last. In 1930 he produced *Rushlight* and in 1931, *Spotlight*.

right
***Flight* at Horning.**

photo: Ken. Clabburn

far right
***Rushlight*.**

photo: Peter Tracey

Herbert Woods bought this trophy with *Flight's* winnings during her first season.

photo: Jennifer Woods

Barton Regatta 1929.

William Jermy sailing *Pintail*. The wherry is *Cornucopia*. The large flag above her Jenny Morgan is a 'winners flag' and indicates she had won the wherry race.

photo: Hugh Tusting

right
***Rushlight* and *Flight*.**

photo: Stewart Morris collection

far right
Gerald Sturgess and his fiancee, Betty Chittock sailing *Swallow*.

photo: cover 1973 NPC Handbook

Hickey.

photo: courtesy East
Anglian Cruising Club

In 1930, C.E.Howard built himself *Hickey,* which became number 11 in the class. She has never raced but can usually be seen moored near the Pleasure Boat at Hickling. In the photograph she's being sailed by Charlie Howard and his great-nephew Cecil Howard. In 1947, Cecil and his brother Bert founded the Green Wyvern Sailing Club and latterly Cecil became a stalwart of the River Cruiser Class. The family could be nicely described as eccentric; a pencilled note on this photograph indicated that Great Uncle Charlie believed the earth to be flat. Right up to his death Cecil was asked to present the Cecil Howard Memorial trophy for River Cruisers, sailed on the River Yare as a 'feeder race' for the the Yare Navigation Race.

far left
Even old lugsails find a use in cold weather. Stewart Morris is standing on the right on Hickling Broad.

photo: Stewart Morris
collection

left
George Fitt rowing two out of three of the Misses Fitt across Barton Broad.

photo: Hugh Tusting

Uffa Fox built his only Norfolk Punt, *Stint,* for Sir Edward Stracey of Rackheath Hall
in 1929. He joined two sections of mast together with duralium tubing (like a fishing
rod, as he had on his famous 14 *Avenger* the previous year) and *Stint* became the first
bermudan rigged punt. She was built to the minimum length of sixteen feet, as Uffa
was confident she would win on corrected time. (Time allowance was twelve seconds
per foot l.o.a.) There is an apocryphal Potter Heigham story about Uffa racing *Stint*
from Potter to the Pleasure Boat at Hickling against Herbert Woods, presumably in
Flight. Uffa failed to win on corrected time and folklore has Woods wagering a fiver
that he could still beat Uffa back to Potter without a rudder - steering with his sails.
Herbert Woods was said to have retained the fiver for some time!

Uffa Fox
*photo: Stewart Morris
collection*

Uffa had many local customers and returned to race *Spotlight* at Potter Heigham
regatta in 1931 but he never really came to terms with Norfolk Punts which; in view of
his involvement with International Canoes, was a lost opportunity. He had developed
an expensive method of construction using double skinned, Honduras mahogany,
separated with canvas (later oiled silk), with Canadian rock elm timbers on two inch
centres throughout the hull. By the standards of the day, the results were fast and stiff
but only the wealthy were able to afford them. Gerald Sambrooke Sturgess later wrote
that Uffa thought of Norfolk Punts as "heavy and sailed by marshmen in thigh boots"
but it seems more likely that he saw a small class that included a number of amateur
built boats with a price effectively restricted to £60. Building twenty two foot punts can
hardly have seemed attractive, when his fourteen foot dinghies fetched over £150.
Doubtless it was coincidental that several punt owners also kept large motor cruisers
at the yards that built their Norfolk Punts. Uffa was again approached after the Second
World War to design a Norfolk Punt but sold his customer an International 10 sq.
metre canoe. The canoe frightened the poor man so much, he disposed of it cheaply to
a young enthusiast after less than a season.

In 1930, the class introduced sail numbers, although their allocation wasn't entirely
logical. The commodore ensured *Shrimp* became number 1. *Prawn* was allocated
number 19, as Harold Morris had shipped an old rig from his Restricted Norfolk 14,
Take-a-Step. George Fitt took sail number 21 for *Flight* for the same reason. Once the
National 14 class was established, the Norfolk fleet was allocated a new block of
numbers: 38 - 60. It may have been expedient but it took the Norfolk Punt class
several years to fill in the inevitable gaps. The annual meeting that year spent some
time trying to decide whether handicaps should be based on length or performance.

Start of the Sundog Cup race at the Norfolk Punt Club regatta at Hickling in 1930.

left to right the Punts are: - *Stint, Bittern, Scoulton Cob, Swallow, Rushlight, Prawn, Flight, Pochard, Swift.*

photo: Stewart Morris collection

left
Prawn sets a spinnaker.

right
Prawn well reefed on Wroxham Broad. The family wherry *Sundog* is in the background of both shots.

photos: Stewart Morris collection

The Broads regatta seasons continued as busily as ever. The Norfolk Punt class raced for the Ardea trophy at Potter Heigham, which had been presented by Howard Hollingsworth. *Ardea* was a large pleasure wherry, built for Hollingsworth as a job creation scheme in 1927 by Leo Robinson at Oulton Broad - he chose the latin name of a heron for his new boat. She was sixty five feet long and built from teak rather than local oak. *Ardea* was taken to Paris in 1959 to provide living accommodation but returned to the Broads in 2005 having spent most of her life in France. Her lines are very slightly different to a traditional wherry and gnarled old hands were heard muttering after her launch: "You can't steam teak".

The Ardea trophy, won outright by Herbert Woods in 1933.
photo: Jennifer Woods

Ardea
photo: Claud Hamilton

Herbert Woods in *Spotlight* at Potter Heigham regatta.

photo: Jennifer Woods

Herbert Woods built *Spotlight* for the 1931 season. He helmed her first race himself but R.O.Bond, a Norwich architect and a successful sailor at both local and national events, was a regular 'jockey' in many of Woods boats. Later in his life, Bond became doyen of the Lowestoft Dragon fleet and served as commodore of the Royal Norfolk & Suffolk Yacht Club for several years.

The same year, the class joined the Norfolk Dinghy Club for their passage race from Horning to Thurne. The Norfolk Punt Club held their regatta at the Horning Town Sailing Club and were responsible for running a days racing during Wroxham Week, which continued for many years after the formation of the Norfolk Broads Y.C.

Herbert Woods
photo: Jennifer Woods

1932 witnessed the first rumblings over hull measurement. *Spotlight* was found to have a rise of floor of 4⅞" instead of 3⅓" and her overall beam had increased by 2". *Swallow* had a rocker of 3⅞" instead of a maximum 3". Both boats had measured when they were built and the committee accepted Messrs Woods and Chittock's explanation that the changes may have been caused by supporting the boats on their ends when they were hauled out. No further action was to be taken beyond requiring that all Punts were to be measured every season!

New rules agreed in September 1932, required new punts to measure twenty two feet overall but permitted masts of similar length. Herbert Woods built *Dodman* and *Mickey* to these rules for the 1933 season. *Shuck* and *Pintail* replaced their old tabernacle stepped bamboo masts with longer metal masts, as did *Stannicle* later in the season. Her steel mast was 1⅝" section but the spar folded whilst hoisting at a windy Acle regatta and was replaced with a conventional wooden spar. There were several new boats in the fleet for the 1933 season. William Mollett built *Cavender* and raced her himself for much of the summer. Carrodus noted sniffily that her bright yellow colour was felt not to be in keeping with the the Norfolk Punt tradition. His declaration that *Cavender* was "rigged in accordance with Dr. Manfred Currey's theories" is enough to strike terror and dismay into the hearts of modern yachtsmen.

Robert Bond

photo: Authors collection

Pochard raced at Hickling and despite developments, *Prawn* was still able to win on handicap. At Thurne regatta in 1933, Stewart Morris once again took the silverware; although he had imported some rule bending from the International <u>14</u> fleet. There was great debate over the unmeasured area of her foresail extending aft of the mast. His Morgan Giles <u>14</u> *Clover* was followed by *RIP*, a dinghy that an ailing Harold Morris had ordered from Uffa Fox. The Prince of Wales Cup for International Fourteens was then the UK's premier dinghy competition and Stewart Morris, crewed by his elder brother Jack, became the first Norfolk Punt Club member to win a national event when they won the Prince of Wales Cup in 1932 and 1933, sailing *RIP*.

It wasn't to be long before more of Stewart Morris' Cambridge friends began to race the family fleet of Broads boats. Peter Scott and John Winter began to appear in the results. Beecher Moore (later to become Jack Holt's partner) crewed *Prawn* for the 1933 season. Moore is credited with the first trapeze (which he called the "bellrope") developments on his Thames 'A' rater *Vagabond*. Scott and Winter developed the trapeze to good effect in 14s in 1938. The East Anglian 14 contingent were already strong but Stewart Morris' small group of wealthy friends from Cambridge University came to dominate British dinghy racing for the next twenty years.

far left
R.I.P. sailed by Jack and Stewart Morris.

photo: Stewart Morris collection

W.L. 'Bey' Clabburn was a member of the NPC committee and audited the club's accounts for several years. He served as secretary of the Norfolk & Suffolk Yachting Association for thirty years.

photo: Ken. Clabburn

It's a shame that Potter Heigham regatta has ceased. It was a major competition for the Punt class and a significant local event, now in danger of fading from memory. Charles Carrodus, wrote in his inimitable style from the wherry *Zulu* in 1933:

"No writer yet born has ever done justice to this great festival, or attempted to do so. After studying the subject for years, he gives the results of the sailing matches and the swimming events; then dismisses the rest of the day as baffling description and passes on to the next regatta, feeling like an inadequate scribe. But it is a day of immense crowds, usually not less than 5,000, of huge parking grounds on both sides of the river, of miles of moored yachts on each bank, both above and below the bridge and of a starting line for yacht racing packed with joyous holidaymakers, and crowded more than ever for the swimming. It is all music and gaiety, laughter and cheers and this year it was again a brilliant finish to the Bure season." He went on to record music from a steam organ on one bank, whilst "Captain J.Collier of Norwich Aero Club gave a display of aerobatics. The day ended with fireworks on Mr. Pratt's meadow." There were about fifty entries a day for yacht racing and the results generally carried some familiar names: "Jack Powles of Wroxham won the one oared race, whilst Nat Bircham won the race for skippers in yacht's dinghies belonging to hired craft."

Barrel race at Potter Heigham regatta.

photo: Back to the Broads, David Holmes

As the 1933 season drew to a close the simmering row over hull measurement came to a head. In May, W.F.Jermy, the class measurer had reported that, on measuring the original *Scoter* for admission to the class, he had found her 'spring of bottom' (rocker) was 1½" too great and also that her 'round of bottom' (rise of floor) was too much. *Scoter* was not a new boat and had been built by C.J.Broom of Brundall in 1929. The committee decided that the rocker would have to be reduced to under the maximum three inches and Herbert Woods sketched out a way to achieve this without major structural alteration. Shortly afterwards, *Swallow* and *Rushlight* were re-measured and also found to have excess rocker. Both boats were altered by Herbert Woods and passed by the official measurer. *Swallow* was rebuilt to ensure she measured - something which Gerald Sambrooke Sturgess claimed ruined her performance but Woods fixed tapered lengths of timber under the bows alongside the hog to the other boats to reduce their rocker. When the commodore, Byron V. Noel and vice commodore T.F. Mase saw what Herbert Woods had done to the boats, they refused to accept his interpretation of the rules. A special committee meeting was called, which developed into a long and heated argument. When a vote was finally taken, Herbert Woods won the vote by four votes to three. Both Flag officers immediately resigned their flag rank and membership of the club. The class had certainly got itself into a considerable muddle. *Winkle,* built for Byron V. Noel and resplendent in bright blue paint didn't measure either - the boat had double the permitted rise of floor. *Flight, Mickey, Scoulton Cob* and *Spotlight* were also found to have measurement deficiencies.

Punts that had measured when they were built had gradually developed increased rocker. Hindsight is a wonderful gift and Woods was probably correct that punts were being driven harder than their original, gunter rigged design had allowed. By the same token, it is almost impossible to be objective about boatbuilding standards after so many years. Broads sailing craft were probably built with a twenty five year life expectancy and crucially, the Norfolk Punt class rules intended punts to be built down to a price. A number of local boatbuilders would be amazed if they could see how many of their products were still sailing around the Broads. Barton broad too was changing. The Victorians could see three churches from the broad but the rapidly growing trees were quickly obscuring the view.

Clouds, sails & a big sky. This shot of an Allcomers start looks like a Hickling Regatta during the 1930s. There is no excuse for its inclusion beyond being a nice photograph.

photo: Hugh Tusting

NORFOLK PUNT CLUB.

The 1933 Annual General Meeting saw the resignation of Gerald Sambrooke Sturgess as Honourary Secretary in view of his imminent marriage and the first public airing of the possibility of one design punts. Stewart Morris' proposal that owners who agreed to modify their punts should not face retrospective disqualification was carried unanimously.

S.H. Morris.

The best post script to the measurement fiasco is that the original *Scoter* was finally allowed to join the class in 1967. Renamed *Goldeneye* she was allocated the number 25, originally held by the Grimes *Snipe*.

The Broads Haven Trophy - presented to the class by Herbert Woods in 1932 but withdrawn the following year during the measurement row.

photo: Jennifer Woods

***Goldeneye* in Paul Bown's workshop in 2005, where she has been completely rebuilt for the Rev. Neville Khambatta. Only the top two planks on either side remain of Broom's original work.**

photo: Author

The Norfolk Punt Club had found kindred spirits in the new Norfolk Dinghy Club, another single class club but still only in it's second season. Robert Bond was a leading light and the dinghy club laid on Norfolk Punt races at their fixtures. The two clubs were close enough for Bond to arrange for the Norfolk Dinghy Club to sail a team race against Trent Valley S.C. at Thurne Mouth in Punts. When the possibility arose of a number of punts being outclassed by the Norfolk Punt Club, the Norfolk Dinghy Club debated at their AGM whether to formally adopt the class to provide a home for rejected punts. Robert Bond was in favour and George Fitt declared that "Punts offered sailing at the same speed as a rater at half the cost." In the event, Cdr. Newcombe persuaded the dinghy club to wait and see. The debate clearly demonstrates not only the vulnerability of single class clubs but also how closely interwoven the Broads clubs were at the time. Cdr. Newcombe's daughter, Rosemarie Lincoln, raced her Norfolk Dinghy *Mardler* for another sixty five years.

The measurement row limited club activity during 1934 but all restrictions on mast height were removed. William Mollett built *Blue Dar* for E.N.Adcock and Herbert Woods produced *Sardine* for Captain C.B.Wilson of Irstead Lodge. Apart from the ill-starred *Stint*, *Sardine* was the first punt to have a properly built bermudan rigged mast with internal halyards and winches. The Wilson family entertained the club to lunch on the lawn at Irstead Lodge, which overlooked the south end of the Broad. The lunch became an annual occasion and food was delivered in hampers by Fortnum and Mason. Free flowing alcohol is reported to have made performances in the afternoon races "variable."

Tom Scott crewing Capt. Wilson in *Sardine*.

photo: Peter Tracey

Irstead Lodge subsequently burnt down but Capt. Charles Wilson claimed to own part of Barton Broad. The rest of the broad was claimed by Leslie Storey, who lived in a large house called 'Burefield', beside Horning church. The house had immaculate gardens running down to the river, set out like a willow pattern plate. Even the tie-bars in the quayheading ended in the letter 'S'. Passers by sometimes caught a glimpse of some strange animals in the garden that presumably helped to keep the acres of grass down. They were described as 'Shoats'; a cross between a sheep and a goat. Happily for the Norfolk Punt Club, both men were keen yachtsmen.

Burefield.

photo: Authors collection

If 1934 saw reduced turnouts for racing, it also witnessed another epic voyage by a Norfolk Punt. Lt. Cdr. S.A.Brookes RN, on leave from Singapore, decided to circumnavigate the rivers Wensum and Bure with his wife in *Bittern*. The trip was written up by the Eastern Daily Press on June 27th & 28th 1934, reproduced by Julia Carter in the 1977 club handbook and here with the Editor's permission.

"*Bittern* is a 20' sailing punt with a beam of no more than 4'10", a draught of four inches and as to tonnage, she taxes the the lifting power of four strong men. Sail area is 160 square feet and the centreplate weighs 49lbs. She was designed for mudlarking as well as for racing and built for us by Alfred Pegg & Sons, five years ago. She has proved herself far too solid and heavy for racing but splendid for sailing in heavy weather. It was after my husband's return from Singapore in April that he had the brainwave of doing this trip. We were sailing on Barton and in some danger of capsizing - when he suggested it and soon we had made all the preparations to leave Norwich for the upper reaches of Wensum, returning home by the upper reaches of the Bure.

Bittern was taken by lorry to Norwich and launched by kind permission of Mr. Anderson from his garden, which was the nearest suitable place we could find to City Station (Queens Road, Norwich, currently the site of Sainsbury's Brazengate store). We carried two sleeping bags, a tent, spare clothing, food and cooking gear, so there hardly seemed room for us.

We set off at about five o'clock, paddling past the Wensum and Swan baths and had our first pull out at Hellesdon, where a hard slope had been specially built for boats, as this is apparently a common hunting ground for Norwich rowers. It turned very cloudy, a cold and miserable night. We took turns in towing along the banks which were piled with mud from recent dredging. We stopped in some woods when tired out.

The boat was too full even for a bicycle pump, so my pneumatic mattress was inflated by cheek-bursting. I tried to sleep in the punt but rolled off the mattress, hit myself on the centre-board casing and felt a martyr. It was a cold, windy morning and I washed *Bittern* down - mud everywhere. Sailing was impossible, as reefing was necessary and she would have got so wet that everything on board would have suffered - this meant towing along the muddy banks and through high nettles. The scenery improved and we met no other craft, which we found an enjoyable change from the lower rivers.

Near Costessey we struck our first bad patch of mud and found towing through it very hot work in the mid-day sun; there were thousands of tadpoles in the shallows and mayfly on the water.

After a laborious haul out at Costessey (unaided except by rollers and a tackle) we sailed to the village; all the ducks and swans fled in alarm in front of us. At the inn we saw a marvellous mug fashioned like a skull. It was German and was brought from the canteen of the Death's Head Hussars. The inn keeper had a fine collection of medals and regimental accoutrements.

Lt. Cdr. Sam Brookes RN, later of Transatlantic and Bermuda race fame learned to sail in *Bittern*, a punt owned by his father. These photographs have been scanned from the Eastern Daily Press of the day. Old newspaper photographs regrettably no longer reflect today's standards of reproduction.

photos:
Eastern Daily Press

I fell asleep while steering, so we pulled up close to Taverham and made camp in a lovely meadow. We found our way to Capt. Lloyd's for permission to pull out next morning and he was most kind and helpful. That night S. slept in the punt and I in the tent. I broke all the rules of camping by taking a hot water bottle to bed. Taverham Mill, now disused is a very pretty place; we passed onto the hills and trees of Ringland and the scenery was topping. We talked to the people in their riverside gardens and they seemed very surprised to see a boat. S. asked about fishing and was told that trout were common: he discussed suitable flies, suggesting mayfly but was told that "a good old lugworm is the best."

Ringland ford was the first part (of many) that was so shallow that we had to get out and push. Soon after this we met our first barbed-wire obstruction - strands of wire fitted across the river to prevent cattle wandering upstream, and shortly after this three trees fallen right across the river. Our pleasant camp at Attlebridge was marred by great pain from the nettle stings, which kept me awake all night. From here to Lenwade we found many more shoals, crowds of nettles, more low bridges and a very low tree across the river, but the countryside was very pretty.

While at Lenwade, by kind permission of Mr. Bullard, S. spent many hours waving a fishing rod but owing to lack of either skill or lugworms, he failed to provide a trout for supper. Though the inn and mill were Lenwade, the post-office, only a hundred yards away was Great Witchingham. We had a difficult pull out past the mill but willing help and a wheel barrow lessened the labour. The country between Lenwade and Lyng was the most beautiful of the whole trip, and we reached by evening an ideal camping spot in private ground by Lyng mill. We went to two village inns to listen to Norfolk talk and found them to be "kitchen inns" - that is having no bar at all. We had camped very near the fall and the noise of the water was like a gale of wind all night. I was warned against rats and bats in my tent but was only disturbed by nettle stings. Lyng is fascinating - the mill pool has a superstition, that when foam comes down it means there will be death to someone in the village abutting the opposite bank; the shape of the foam indicates whether the person is a man, woman or child. We had a fairly easy pull out and easy towing to Elsing Mill. Here we pulled out again and had a painful trip to Swanton Morley, towing through banks of high nettles. We camped again at the "fall" of the demolished mill; again there was water rushing down all night and this with the sound of the wind in the trees of a nearby copse was quite eerie. On the next morning after much calculation, we hauled *Bittern* up a ten foot bank, through the copse and into the river. It was a great achievement but a heavier task than we should have attempted alone. We went along, towing nearly all the way and the nettles were terrible again. The country was pretty but flattish, the weather gloriously warm and the wind had dropped. We bathed and shopped at Billingford, a tiny, pretty village, which seemed fast asleep in the sunshine. We camped in sight of Watt's Naval training School and much enjoyed visiting it the next day.

Having learned to respect the nettles I did my share of the towing to North Elmham Mill with bandages worn under two pairs of stockings. Beyond this mill which was very busy we were soon reminded of a warning about weeds stopping us, for we got to the mill boom and found a years accumulation blocking the way. They were nearly as solid as soil and the smell was terrible when we carved a way through with a paddle.

We had a pretty trip - many shallows and much weed, but nothing bad till we came to wire netting across the river. This was so weighted down by weed that we were able to force *Bittern* over it and then had a glorious view of Bintree Mill and a large rock garden ablaze with colour. The miller told us we were the first people up there in a boat for years, but he had helped many over long ago. I was so tired I rested in the house, whilst S. and willing helpers pulled the punt over. From here to Ryburgh was terribly difficult; the weeds were very thick and and the banks were full of nettles or cows. I found towing most unpleasant and we were both very hot and tired. We got through a most difficult broken down bridge and soon after arrived at Great Ryburgh mill. It was blowing hard and very cold and we soon had a hot meal and turned in.

The next day we laxed, after having moved the punt into the upper stream. At the inn we listened to the talk and played darts (this inn has three glorious settles, all very old). It was a very cold night and the noise of the wind and falling water scared me stiff. The last lap to Fakenham was on a lovely but very windy day. The towing was easy for long stretches. The country was pretty but not hilly. I hurriedly gave up towing to S. when I was near about forty young bulls; they were so curious about us that they followed S. along the bank to the fence, where they crowded over each other to get a good, last look at us. Then we came to a difficult snag across the river, a boom sticking just above the water with wire netting from this to the river bed and across it. All heavy gear had to be taken out and put in again when we had cleared the obstruction. We had five of these within a short distance and were terribly tired. When we reached Fakenham, we had to go under such a low footbridge that it scraped the coaming of the punt. We camped in a field belonging to the garage which had undertaken to remove *Bittern* to Saxthorpe on the upper Bure. So many people had told us we wouldn't make it to Fakenham that we could hardly believe we were there - nine days out from Norwich. Next morning there was great difficulty getting *Bittern* on board the lorry which was only twelve feet long on the floor - she was lashed with her bow cocked up over the driving cab and so away through driving mist and rain to Saxthorpe for our return journey. We arrived at 11.00 a.m. and found there was little water in the stream as the mill was not running. I had news from home which necessitated my leaving at once for Wroxham. and S. decided to carry on alone until I was able to rejoin him. He promised to keep a log of his movements and here it is: -

"I waited till the mill was started at 1400 when I was able to push *Bittern* downstream half afloat - about two miles to Itteringham, where I arrived at 1900. In this lap, I waded almost all the way as the water would not float me on board and in some places I had to place rollers on the river bottom to float *Bittern*. I actually passed eleven barbed wire fences across the river, went under three fallen trees and two shallow footbridges, which were a very close fit. The boat jammed badly between one of the trees and and the hard bed of the river, and it was only by carving the bark of the tree that I at last got her through. The miller and his sons helped me at Itteringham, and we moved her that evening. Next morning I was away early with the river keeper in company. His help in wading boots was invaluable, as my feet were sore after yesterday's work, and we made Blickling mill in the early afternoon, after a short but very pleasant 'nap' in Blickling Woods - the most perfect spot I have met in the whole trip.

My next halt was at Ingworth, and rain delayed progress for two days. I eased the punt down through the disused mill sluice on a rope, an anxious job but she went through splendidly. I soon got to Aylsham and on the miller's advice took the canal in preference to the main river, and found it good and deep with a helpful current; it was however terribly narrowed by reeds and in places it was all I could do to force through them. Suddenly I came upon the lock, concealed by undergrowth and far out in the country with no habitation in sight. The upper gates had almost disappeared in decay but the lower ones were more robust - the stream was running through a hole in one of them, which was not quite large enough for *Bittern* to scrape through. The banks were high and the land very rough for pulling her out and round, in fact I felt defeated. After some deliberation, I decided to try and open the gate. With the mainsheet and bow ropes, I rigged a single whip on the gate itself from a fallen tree and put the jigger on this. I could only just muster enough rope but it did the trick - the gate was partly silted up and took some moving, but at last I got it open wide enough and slipped through, arriving next at Burgh."

Here I joined S. with his great friend Fred, and we found our progress and portage much easier than when we were alone. There was a great difference in travelling downstream and in glorious sunshine, we towed easily to Oxnead mill, where we pulled out quite simply and paddled to Buxton mill. The river was still shallow and weedy and both banks were swampy, so we camped near Horstead. We were now on the fringe of civilisation, and the inn at Horstead did not seem so villagey as those higher up. We bought a lovely old beer mug and played darts.

At Horstead Mill we learned that there had been such trouble from people in boats that there was talk of opening up all the locks; if so it was feared that the upper reaches would be ruined by the rowdy element of the visitors. At last after many days of enforced idleness the sails could be used again. We stopped at Coltishall to look at the new weed cutter alongside the village inn, and then sailed to Wroxham ending our cruise at the bottom of our garden. Two bolts have been torn out of *Bittern's* bow; the bottom was badly scraped but otherwise, she stood the trip splendidly." This wasn't quite the end of *Bittern's* adventures that year. Before Lt. Cdr. Brooke's leave ran out, the couple sailed *Bittern* to Acle and up the Muck Fleet to Filby Broad.

Harold Morris, the club's founding commodore, had been ill since 1931 and died in 1935. The family fleet was sold and Stewart began to race at Itchenor. His uncle, Eric Morris who had owned *Trout* and the Brown boat *Spoonbill* also began to sailing on the South Coast. *Spoonbill* was taken to Chichester harbour, where she fitted with a bermudan rig for Allcomers racing.

The club bought a Harland and Wolff lifeboat, which was converted to a houseboat by Cox Bros at Barton Turf and contained lockers and facilities for landing from the very low freeboard of a Norfolk Punt. During the 1936 season, the houseboat remained at Ant Mouth until mid June when she was towed back to Barton for the remainder of the season bar Wroxham Week.

Charles Carrodus again:

"Today a fresh northeasterly wind on these open waters but full sail is set. The course for the first race is from Ant Mouth to Thurne Mouth, and the commodore's launch is seen about one o'clock running down the river to fix the buoy at the turning point. Six punts turn up for the open meeting, a good number for so early in the season near this rather bleak coast. Among them is Mr. & Mrs. Peter Cator's new boat, *Gamecock*. Unfortunately the rigging requires some adjustment and to the great disappointment of all present they are unable to sail. With her varnished mahogany hull, cream decks, Bermuda mast and sail and hollow spars, she is a fine looking punt and gives every indication of speed. We shall look forward to her maiden race.

With Mrs. Wilson, the wife of the commodore, officiating at the stop watch and time sheets, a good start is made for the first race at 2.46, all getting away well. In fact in the case of *Blue Dar*, sailed by her new owners, Mr. H. and Miss Cicely Bolingbroke, a little too well as she is over the line and is recalled. However she comes about smartly, restarts and is soon in the running. The outward journey involves close hauling all the way with a little tacking. *Sardine* and *Rushlight* are well in front, and making a race of it when a crack is heard, and *Sardine's* mast is seen to go overboard, which of course finishes the race as far as she is concerned. Capt. C.B.Wilson was sailing with Mr. G.Sambrooke Sturgess as crew, and making the best of a bad job, hauling their sail out of the water and making ready for a tow back to the houseboat, they are passed by the other boats. Apparently the smash occurred through a diamond giving way and Captain Wilson's launch is soon on the spot to tow her home.

Caister Maid **was was owned by A.T.Chittock.** *Swallow I* **is alongside and Gerald Sambrooke Sturgess is standing on the side deck.**

photo: Judy Macdonald (nee Sturgess) and Peter Sturgess

Dr. Tracey, the new owner of *Rushlight* wins the race easily saving his handicap on *Stannicle* by 1 min. 4 secs. for the four and a half miles. *Stannicle.* sailed by the secretary, Mr. Eric Chamberlin and *Blue Dar* have a most exciting race, passing and repassing each other five or six times, *Blue Dar* eventually overhauling *Stannicle* almost on the line, beating the amateur built boat by a foot."

The same year saw the launch of probably the most influential Norfolk Punt ever built. Herbert Woods designed and built *Swallow II* for Gerald Sambrooke Sturgess and his father in law, A.T.Chittock. The pair were to own her until 1960. After their experiences rebuilding the first *Swallow, Swallow II* became the first punt to be designed with her centreplate and rudder casing contained in a single, box-section down her centreline to prevent any movement from her designed rocker. She set a parachute spinnaker and was the first Norfolk Punt to fit a kicking strap and a snubbing winch for the jib.

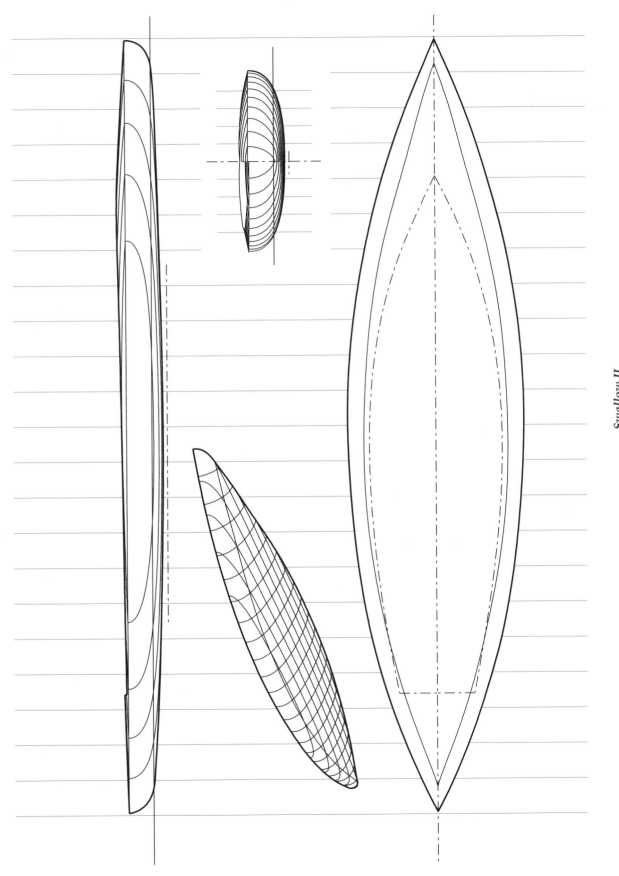

Swallow II

Drawn by Andrew Wolstenholme for J.M.Evans from measurements taken by Paul Bown and reproduced with their kind permission

right
Rosybill.

far right
Swallow II.

photos:
courtesy Mike Evans

The Norfolk Punt logo made its first public appearance as the front cover of the 1936 club handbook. This splendid piece of unattributed graphics may originally have been a woodcut.

far right
A Tracey family card from 1936.

right
A start at Barton during the same season.

photos:
courtesy Peter Tracey

On the Right Tack.
Rushlight, July 1936.

The 1936 Olympics provided the young club with its first real international successes. The single handed dinghy selected for the 1936 games, sailed at Kiel in August of that year, was the specially designed Olympic Monotype. Stewart Morris had trouble getting on with the boat but attended as reserve to Peter Scott. This was the last occasion when two entries per country were permitted - the German number two was detailed to ram his colleague's rivals; despite his own inevitable disqualification. The ploy failed and The Netherlands scraped Gold from Germany with Scott in the Bronze position for Great Britain.

Chris Boardman in
Lalage's **helmsmans**
cockpit.

photo: Uffa Fox

Chris Boardman, owner of *Shrimp* and a Norfolk Punt Club member since 1929, provided the greatest cause for celebration. Together with Capt. Russell Harmer (father of Tom) he took the Gold medal in the Six Metre class, sailing K51 *Lalage*.

The oak tree presented to gold medal winners at these Olympics was planted at the family home at How Hill with due ceremony. It's known as the 'Hitler Oak' and can still be seen in the garden, although an explanatory notice has been removed in an assertion of political correctness over history.

Lalage.

photo: Uffa Fox

Capt. Russell Harmer's
Olympic gold medal.

photographed by courtesy of
Tom Harmer

By the end of 1936, the club had largely overcome it's internal difficulties and seventeen punts of varying sizes competed in sixty three races, making a total of four hundred and sixty nine starts with an average turnout of seven boats. Membership had risen to eighty six and the first Prize Giving Dinner was held at the Thatched Cottage Restaurant in Norwich. The building had once been used as an elaborate dance hall and Bonds department store (now John Lewis) was built on the site.

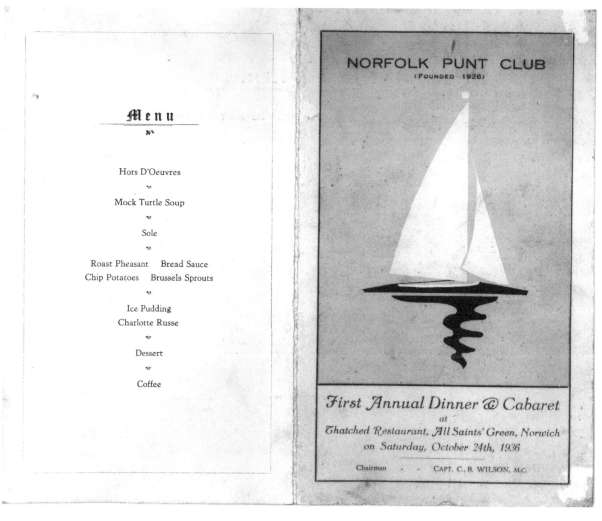

above
1936 Annual Dinner menu

courtesy: Jane de Quincey

right
The Thatched Restaurant.

photo: Authors collection

Toast List.

Cabaret Items by "The Rafters" under the direction of Jack Lamb.

To Propose			To Respond
The Commodore		"THE KING"	Everyone

──────── INTERVAL ────────

	Autopical Trio	"MARCHING ON"	"The Rafters"
Capt. Trubshawe		"THE NORFOLK PUNT CLUB"	The Commodore (Capt. C. B. Wilson, M.C.)
	A Song	"KING OF THE ROAD"	Basil Platten
	Humorous Item	"CASTLES IN THE AIR"	Miss Pearl Keymer
A. T. Chittock, Esq.		"THE FLAG OFFICERS"	The Rear-Commodore (Dr. B. M. Tracey)
	A Song	"THE CLUB SONG" (With apologies to "Phil The Fluter")	Eric Chamberlin, A.V.C.M.
	Nothing in particular	Introducing	Jack Lamb
The Vice-Commodore (A. L. Russell, Esq.)		"THE VISITORS"	Com. J. H. Montgomery, R.N. R. J. May, Esq.
	Character Trio	"TOPPER - BOWLER - CAP"	We Three

Presentation of Prizes by Mrs. C. B. WILSON.

	Another Song	By	Basil Platten
	Ventriloquial Nonsense and Mimicry	"THE YOUNG FATHER," etc.	Eric Chamberlin, A.V.C.M.
	In Lighter Vein	AN IMPRESSION	Miss Pearl Keymer
	An Interrupted Duet	Introducing	Jack and Basil
	A Final Item	"TAKING OUR LEAVE"	"The Rafters"

GOD SAVE THE KING

At the Piano - J. F. Blyth.

Eric Chamberlin worked at Herbert Woods yard at Potter Heigham and served for many years as club secretary. He gave his first rendition at the dinner of his Norfolk Punt Club song, to the tune of 'Phil the Fluter':

"Do you know the Norfolk Punt Club that sails on Barton Broad?
A happy lot of sporting folk the angels will reward,
They cluster round the houseboat like seagulls on a rock
But one fine day they'll tip her up and get an awful shock.
First we'll take the commodore, he's handsome and equitable,
He has a lovely *Sardine* that has never seen a tin,
His lady's kind and gracious and exceedingly hospitable,
And the claret cup at Irstead Lodge, it helps you on to win.

So point her up and haul your wind, get ready for the gun
But never set your spinnaker until you're on the run.
Though some may ride and some may shoot, while others like to hunt
The finest sport in all the world is sailing in a punt.

There's Dr. Basil Tracey, he's both capable and keen.
He rushes *Rushlight* round the Broad, her tail is seldom seen.

He likes to chat of this and that and things that interest him,
Until a gentle voice is heard "it's time to come home, Tim."
And Russell racing *Cavender,* his lady crewing dutifully,
Chasing Peter Cator, who says starboard with a yell,
With 'Kytie' on the tiller making *Gamecock* travel beautifully.
Then Jermy starts a luffing match and sells his punt as well.

So point her up and haul your wind, get ready for the gun
But never set your spinnaker until you're on the run.
Though some may ride and some may shoot, while others like to hunt
The finest sport in all the world is sailing in a punt.

There's Gerald Sambrooke Sturgess, he's both elegant and trim,
And complicated handicaps are nothing much to him.
And he can cure your toothache, he's a man of many parts,
And he decorates the houseboat with thing-me-bobs and charts,
And Wedderburn and Andrews racing *Pintail* with tenacity,
To catch the brothers Bolingbroke - sailing in *Blue Dar.*
Wedderburn likes swimming and he dives with great audacity
To rescue damsels in distress when overturned they are.

So point her up and haul your wind, get ready for the gun
But never set your spinnaker until you're on the run.
Though some may ride and some may shoot, while others like to hunt
The finest sport in all the world is sailing in a punt.

Now when the racing's over and the wind is falling light,
We take tea on the houseboat where the conversations bright.
Then Mrs Arendt mothers us and rations out the cake,
She superintends the washing up and keeps us all awake.
We've lots more boats and owners, all with fascinating qualities
To chatter of the lot of them would take up too much time,
So thank you very much for putting up with my fribilities.
I really had an awful job to get the words to rhyme.

So point her up and haul your wind, get ready for the gun
But never set your spinnaker until you're on the run.
Though some may ride and some may shoot, while others like to hunt
The finest sport in all the world is sailing in a punt."

**Wroxham Week 1937.
l to r**

**Messrs. Wedderburn
and Andrews in** *Pintail,*
Peter Cator in
Gamecock, **John Curl in**
Decoy **and Gerald
Sturgess sailing**
Swallow II.

*photo:
courtesy Mike Evans*

The 1937 AGM discussed a proposal that the Norfolk Punt Club amalgamate with the Great Yarmouth Y.C. (founded in 1883), the Norfolk Dinghy Club (1931), the Horning Town Sailing Club (1910) and the Yare & Bure Sailing Club (1876) to form a new club to be known as the Norfolk Broads Yacht Club. This club intended to take on a lease of Wroxham Broad, which was seen as a considerable opportunity by many sailors for racing on private water with private, shorebased facilities away from a growing number of hire boats. Horning Sailing Club was founded the day Horning Town S.C. members decided to amalgamate into the new club at Wroxham. It is interesting to reflect that many H.T.S.C. members considered Horning Reach too crowded for sensible racing even in those days. The formation of the NBYC marked the beginning of Broads sailing clubs feeling a need for on-shore facilities and the inception of the territorial aspirations that clubs hold today. Probably an unconsidered side effect of the new club was an erosion of existing clubs ability to organise regattas when and where they felt like, virtually anywhere on the river system.

Most local yachtsmen belonged to most local sailing clubs and the debate must have revealed a number of divided loyalties. Despite strong support in some quarters, the Norfolk Punt Club declined the invitation to amalgamate and by fifteen votes to five, elected to remain at Barton. As the Norfolk Broads Yacht Club was formed, the Norfolk Punt Club found itself the third oldest sailing club in the area to the Royal Norfolk & Suffolk Y.C. (1859) and the Beccles Amateur S.C. founded in 1902.

None of the punts built after *Swallow II* had improved on her performance and the class began to feel that the future might best be served by adopting a new Herbert Woods designed, carvel built, one-design hull. The decision was, wisely as it turned out, fudged. Any prospective builder would be free to build to the old rules if they wished and choice of rig and equipment was left to the existing class rules. Woods was given the freedom to design the new hull outside the existing class rules if he felt he could improve on *Swallow II's* performance. The specification and plans were agreed in December 1938 and adopted at a meeting in the Thatched Restaurant.

Uffa Fox produced a series of five yachting books during the 1930s. The sixth in the series was overtaken by the Second World War but John Leather found these immaculate drawings of Herbert Woods' One Design Norfolk Punt amongst Uffa's papers and intended for inclusion in the still-born, sixth volume.

John maintains the drawings are unlikely to be by either Uffa or Herbert Woods. He included them in his own work 'Sail and Oar'.

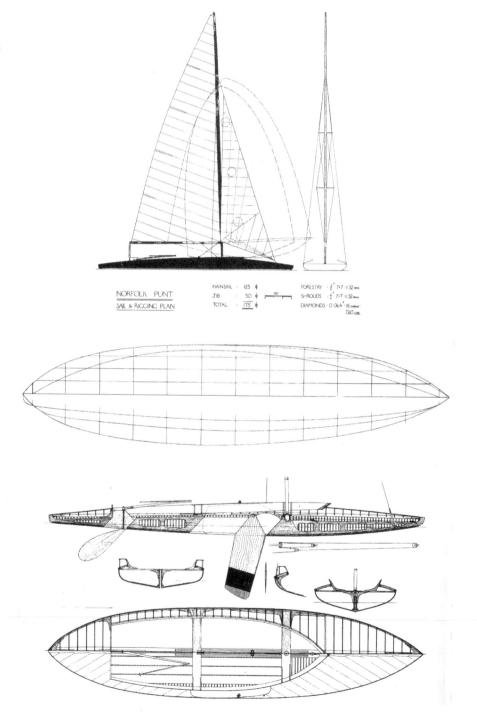

NORFOLK PUNT

SAIL & RIGGING PLAN

MAINSAIL · 125
JIB · 50
TOTAL · 175

FORESTAY · 7×7 ·1·32
SHROUDS · 7×7 ·1·32
DIAMONDS · 0·064 · 16

Herbert Woods produced three boats to his new design. *Kipper* was built for W.G.Jones and Frank Beaching. *Bloater* (now *Curlew*) for Eric Chamberlin and *Limelight* he kept for himself.

Limelight.

photo: Jennifer Woods

The class had come to expect every new Herbert Woods' punt to be faster than the last and *Limelight's* first outing was keenly awaited. She was towed from Potter Heigham to Hickling for her debut in the 1939 race for the Wortley Bowl. Gerald Sambrooke Sturgess recalled, with more than a hint of self satisfaction:

"He was accompanied to the regatta by his wife and a party of young friends, who, one suspects had come to witness yet another triumph for Herbert. Sadly for them, *Swallow II* beat *Limelight* by nearly two minutes and *Widgeon* beat her by over half a minute. As soon as Herbert finished, he stowed her and went straight back to Potter Heigham. It seems doubtful that any champagne corks popped there! *Swallow II* had a successful day with a hat-trick, which must have been even more galling, in thus emulating Herbert's own earlier performances."

The Wortley Cup Hickling Broad 1939.

l to r
Widgeon **(W.F.Jermy)**
Limelight **(Herbert Woods) and** *Swallow II* **(A.T.Chittock).**

photo: courtesy Mike Evans

Swallow II at Wroxham in 1939 - from a montage on the menu for the Norfolk Broads Yacht Club's Annual dinner.

International political pressure increased and the 1939 Broads regatta season progressed uneasily beside the Danzig crisis. Contemporary reports are overwhelmed with an air of unreality and knowledge of the inevitability of another war. The season was nearly done when the Second World War was declared; half way through Lowestoft Sea Week.

Punts were stored as far out of harms way as possible for the duration. Judy Macdonald (nee Sturgess) recalled: "At the outbreak of war *Swallow II* was put up on blocks in Gilbert Chittock's boathouse at the Rookery, Dilham - an afternoon I can remember vividly although I was only three and a half!"

Chapter 3
Post War & Plywood

The 1946 club AGM was held at the Lamb Inn, Orford Place, Norwich in February and attended by fifteen members. The meeting was told that the club had lost Peter Beard (*Rosybill*), John Curl (*Decoy*), Dr. Stephen Falla, Ivan Green (*Smee*), Charles Hanbury Williams and John Wilson (*Sardine*), all of whom had died on active service. C.S.Robinson (*Scoulton Cob*) had been killed off Norway. John Curl had been lost flying over the North Sea and at the meeting his brother Henley announced that *Decoy* had been sold to John Abbott for £100 and it had been his brother's wish that the proceeds be donated to the Norfolk Punt Club. Mr.W.H.Scott presented the club with *Boy William*, their family launch in memory of his son Tom. It was to be another three years before *Boy William* hit the highlights of her own petrol ration.

John Abbott racing *Decoy* at Barton regatta in 1946. A rotating mast had been fitted to replace her pre-war 'birdcage' rigging.

photo: John Abbott

The open hull purchased in 1938 and club houseboat had both been taken over by the Admiralty and in common with a number of yachts, left moored on Barton Broad for the duration of the war to prevent an expected landing by German seaplanes. After five years of neglect they were in terrible condition. Barton had been closed for the duration but the authorities had been persuaded to permit sailing on Wroxham Broad. Most punt sailors not on active service lived in Norwich and for several years they had enjoyed more sailing per petrol coupon by racing with the Norfolk Broads Y.C.

There were two major hurdles to be overcome before the Norfolk Punt Club could make any attempt to continue as it had before the war. The club had only forty six members and even a club handbook was considered "out of the question" for the year. It was decided to ask the Norfolk Broads Y.C. to continue to put on races for Norfolk Punts in the first and last third of the season and to join with Horning Sailing Club and the East Anglian Cruising Club for racing at Thurne Mouth during the mid-part of the season. The club ran a full day during Wroxham Week and rented the club houseboat to other clubs at Thurne Mouth. In 1946, Capt. Wilson and Leslie Storey transferred their ownership of Barton Broad to the Norfolk Naturalists Trust and some members felt that by not organising racing at Barton, the club's right to do so might lapse by default. Peter Cator approached Anthony Buxton of the Naturalists Trust, who agreed to allow the club to continue to sail on the Broad, free of mooring fees but in return hoped for a donation to their own funds.

The second problem facing a club dedicated to Norfolk Punts was the availability of punts. Prices quoted for new boats and the scarcity of seasoned timber after the war had made the old designs prohibitively expensive. The club needed something new to ensure the future of the class. Despite the problems, Eric Chamberlin managed to update his Norfolk Punt Club Song for the club dinner:

"Oh it's nice to sail a punt again after all these years;
We've had our share of misery, and blood and sweat and tears,
We've lost some gallant members, but they would not have us sad,
They paid for everything we love with everything they had.
Then here's to sailing Norfolk Punts with lots of joviality,
And happy days at Barton in the years that are to come,
And may the club continue to increase in popularity;
If we pull together folks we're sure to make things hum.

Chorus: So point her up and haul your wind, get ready for the gun,
But never set your spinnaker until you're on the run.
Though some may fish and some may shoot and others like to hunt,
The finest sport in all the world is sailing in a punt.

We've got some new flag officers, all tested, tried and true,
(That's apt alliteration, if you see it as I do.
And plagiarism is a sin we all commit at times,
But if you've had some sherry, you'll forgive the cockney rhymes.)
Ph! Dr. Tracey's commodore, a very gallant medic,
His lady listens patiently to all he has to say,
He's keen as mustard on the club, though given to punctilio,
His cheery personality will help us on our way.

Chorus.

Then Peter Cator's second flag - or better known as "Vice',
He has some startling attributes, his lady's rather nice,
He was a naval officer, patrolling around the Wash,
He kept his crew on tenterhooks by drinking lemon squash.
And next to him is a man of perspicacity,
Paul Andrews is rear commodore, he's last but never least,
His ideas are original and argued with tenacity,
We all congratulate him on his return from the East.

Chorus.

There's secretary Wedderburn, he's better known as John,
He was a gallant Major and a treat to look upon.
The Japs once thought they'd captured him and gave a winning shout,
But he put his thumb up to his nose a spread his fingers out.
Before I say good night, I must pay a little tribute to
Dear old Gerald Sturgess - He's sitting over there,

He ran the club for seven years with plenty else to do,
A very handsome copper with his nose up in the air."

Chorus.

By 1947, the number of punts racing had dropped to about a dozen. In his apparently relentless pursuit of owning a faster punt than *Swallow II*, Basil Tracey ordered *Martin* from Martham, to be built to Herbert Woods design. His son, Peter Tracey advises that Basil never considered the boat a success. Gerald Sturgess had become the country's leading authority on yacht racing rules and later that year was elected to the RYA Council, becoming chairman of the RYA Protest Committee.

Gerald Sambrooke Sturgess.

photo: Yachting World

The Norfolk Punt Club was still in a highly marginal state. Gerald Sturgess served as commodore of the Norfolk Punt Club in 1945/6 and again in 1949/50. He was in favour of the club moving permanently to Wroxham Broad but other members were not so happy about the prospect. As if to compound the connection, he also served as commodore of the Norfolk Broads Yacht Club in 1948.

far left
Basil Tracey sailing a reefed *Martin* on Wroxham Broad in about 1950.
photo: Peter Tracey

left
Paul Bown racing *Martin* at Wroxham 55 years later. Paul rebuilt her in 2005.
photo: Author

The Broads Regatta season continued as if nothing had happened. This crowded start includes four Great Yarmouth One Designs setting their 'pothunter' rigs. In pole position is the old rater *Vixen*. The dismasted punt in their midst probably reflects the crowded conditions.

photo: courtesy Derek Gibbs

Whilst Stewart Morris' connections with Norfolk Punts had become more distant since his father's death, the club revelled in reflected glory when he became the second club member to win an Olympic Gold medal in the Swallow class at Torbay in 1948. Whilst he had beaten the world in the Swallows, the International 14 remained Stewart Morris' first love. He competed in thirty four Prince of Wales Cup races, winning on twelve occasions and finishing in the first six in twenty four of them. A record unlikely to be beaten by today's sailors.

Stewart Morris sailing the Swallow *Swift* **in 1948.**

photo: Beken

1948 found Robert Bond, fresh from the Torbay Olympic trials in his Star *Miranda*, once again at the helm of Herbert Woods *Limelight* for Wroxham Week. It was her first outing since the war. Despite a more modern, single spreader rig and modifications to her bow to "improve her grip" she still struggled to beat *Swallow II*. The one design hulls with their reduced beam could have it their own way in light weather but were unable to hold *Swallow II* in a blow.

Limelight **sporting her new bow.**

photo: Jennifer Woods

Thanks to the enthusiasm of Herbert Woods and through his good offices, use of the Norfolk & Suffolk Yacht Owners Association weed-cutter, Barton Broad received some much needed maintenance in 1949. At that year's Annual General Meeting, held at White's Restaurant in Norwich, there was further debate about how to rejuvenate the club. The Norfolk Punt Club and the Norfolk Punt class had been eponymous but the meeting decided to open the Club to non Punt owners. In future, only one flag officer and four committee members had to be punt owners. This decision recognised the weakness of a single class club and was designed to attract 'ordinary' yachtsmen to Barton. The move had little immediate impact but the foundations for the club's success today had been laid. Confidence was still lacking and the same meeting also debated amalgamation with the newly formed Hickling Broad Sailing Club, returning to Wroxham Broad and a possible amalgamation with the East Anglian Cruising Club at Thurne.

Eric Chamberlin once again did his best to amuse his fellow punt sailors at the club dinner. His songs provide an interesting historical perspective on what was considered significant. By 1950, he had graduated to the tune of 'Much Binding in the Marsh':

"At Much Barton on the Turf,
The Norfolk Punt Club's quite an institution.
At Much Barton on the Turf -
They say we're getting near to destitution.
They say there is no welcome there for people who are new
- our critics I won't mention, as there's only just a few -
they say we have our sails up but we haven't got a clue!
At Much Barton on the Turf.

At Much Barton on the Turf,

the houseboat is our scene of congregation,
At Much Barton on the Turf
We think it quite good accommodation.
It gets a wee bit crowded when it's time to have a pee -
it's best to take your tea outside or on the upper deck -
Inside there's quite a chance you'll get a cupful down your neck!
At Much Barton on the Turf.

At Much Barton on the Turf
Our commodore is Mr. Peter Standley,
- an upright figure, bold and fine and manly.
At after dinner speeches he is nothing less than great,
He drives his car and *Rushlight* too at a tremendous rate;
He's such a damn fine skipper but he really needs a mate.
At Much Barton on the Turf.

At Much Barton on the Turf,
This year has seen some breaking with tradition,
At Much Barton on the Turf,
Though for this sin there's maybe some remission,
The vice - com* is the man to blame. I'll say it to his face -
He broke his old established custom - oh what a disgrace!
- For *Merry Spinner* actually finished in a race!
At Much Barton on the Turf.

At Much Barton on the Turf,
Occasionally we have a few capsizes,
At Much Barton on the Turf,
For this we really don't know who the prize is,+
The Colonel, now rear commodore has drilled us really fine,
What we do now, we do together, smartly, all in time -
We don't turn over one by one - we do it all in line!
At Much Barton on the Turf.

At Much Barton on the Turf,
A famous cup was won by Doctor Basil,
At Much Barton on the Turf,
With *Gently** he got into quite a frazzle,
Out there in front he showed us that *Martin* was no dud,
And when that fellow Clabburn nearly put him on the mud,
We heard him calling: "Water!" but he really wanted blood!
At Much Barton on the Turf.

At Much Barton on the Turf,
We have a man who ought to be in Heaven,
At Much Barton on the Turf,
He's sailed in punts since 1927+;
Regatta day and *Swallow* got behind the blooming lot -
Her skipper, strange to say had got himself into a spot -
But he pulled up his nylon++ - and just walked off with the pot.
At Much Barton on the Turf.

At Much Barton on the Turf,
Though some may say that Punts have had their day, Sir,
At Much Barton on the Turf,
They'll see us out in strength again in May, Sir;

While some may fish and some may shoot and others like to hunt,
And some just sit and contemplate and grow a great big front,
The finest sport in all the world is sailing in a punt!
At Much Barton on the Turf.

[++] *Swallow II was the only punt setting a spinnaker at the time.*

Aerial photograph of the Norfolk Punt Club pontoons at Barton.

photo: Peter Tracey

Another aerial shot of Barton Broad taken when there was still room to walk a dog on the island.

photo: Peter Tracey

Head Keeper Ted Piggins is 'shoving' a sickly King George VI back to Whiteslea after the 1951 Hickling coot shoot. King George was an elegant shot and a regular visitor to Hickling. Few people notice the King is sitting in a carvel sailing punt.

photo: Back to the Broads, David Holmes

Members generally favoured the adoption of *Swallow II* as a one design hull but Herbert Woods' quotation of £300 for building a similar punt was felt too expensive. 'Percy' Percival offered £256 for building a similar punt to *Decoy,* with a reduction for an order for three boats. The club also agreed to approach Wyche and Coppock of Nottingham to enquire about construction of new punts. During the year, Gerald Sambrooke Sturgess talked with Dick Wyche, who had seen no detailed plans but indicated he could probably build an order for three at £250 each. Wyche & Coppock had developed the Graduate dinghy for 'Light Craft' magazine and Dick mentioned, almost in passing that he thought a plywood, hardchine punt would come out cheaper still. Plywood had been produced throughout the war for use in aircraft construction and was much more readily available than seasoned timber.

Dick Wyche.

photo: Mary Wyche

Jack Holt had designed a successful plywood International Canoe and was invited to Wroxham Broad in the autumn of 1951 to sail three of the faster punts. Jack arrived trailing a Hornet, with a crew in the passenger seat and clearly intent on making a sales pitch. They rigged the Hornet and planed off in an impressive volume of spray but were surprised when the punts sailed past to windward and leeward, on every point of sail. A copy of the class rules duly returned to Putney and a half model of a plywood, hardchine punt was produced with a quote for £275 for a single boat and £250 per boat, if three were ordered together. The class still thought prices too high and returned to Dick Wyche. Gerald Sturgess prevailed on Herbert Woods to let him have sight of the drawings for *Swallow II.*

Members were invited to subscribe two hundred and forty shares of £1 each and a new, hardchine plywood punt was built, based on *Swallow II* but with a little more rocker and rise of floor, to accommodate flat panels and straight chines. Best of all, the new design had a bow profile just like a proper gun punt. The price was to be £190 plus £35 for sails. The class desperately needed a shot in the arm, only one new Norfolk Punt had been built in fourteen years. *Scoter*, the new punt was to be put up for sale at the end of her first season.

The plywood Norfolk Punt performed well. She was 100lbs lighter than *Swallow II* and faster in light weather. Dick Wyche's friends at Light Craft magazine ran this review of the new boat. *Scoter* used a set of *Martin's* sails for her sailing trials.

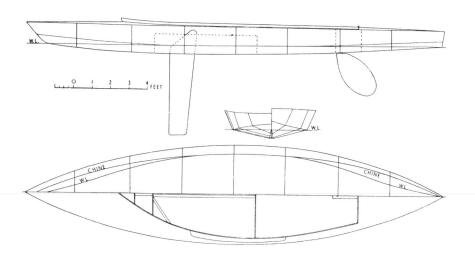

A NEW NORFOLK PUNT

This unique new racing punt gives high performance at a low price—may save the class

REPORT

BY

C. L. NELSON

ONE is apt to think that these are the days of really high-speed sailing boats and the craft sailed by father and grandfather were as whiskery as the owners. Such an opinion could not be leakier and a case in point is the famous racing punt of the Norfolk Broads. This remarkable craft was based on the fenman's gun punt and was developed on the Broads into an out-and-out racing class, the typical boat being a 22-footer of low freeboard, flattish floors, narrow beam, pointed ends and a high narrow sail plan of no less than 176 square feet.

The Norfolk Punt Club with a roving H.Q. consisting of a houseboat, used to stage regular meetings before the war and the craft were famous for their terrific speed. Since the war

Weight of this 20ft. plywood punt's hull is only 200lbs. (Photo: Edward Eves).

This hard chine Norfolk Punt costs little more than half as much as the original design. (Photo : Edward Eves).

however, the cost of building one of these flyers in the traditional manner (clinker above the water, carvel below) has soared to such a height—about £350—that only one of them has been built and the class is threatened with extinction.

Recently the Club was offered a cheaper, modern type of racing craft but the demonstration boat was lapped by one or two of the old-timers and the Club cast around for a builder who would re-design the racing punt and cut down building costs. Dick Wyche of Nottingham was approached and he re-designed the punt using hard chine plywood construction and quoting for a 20 foot, water line boat at £190 less sails. The Club was interested and ordered him to build a prototype—but making one firm stipulation—he was on no account to reduce the sail area.

The other day we had the hair-raising pleasure of attending the new Norfolk Punt's sailing trials. When the prototype was carried down to the rolling waters of the Trent, it resembled nothing so much as a giant

cigar made of wood and split open like a kippered herring to display a central wooden backbone running the whole length of the well. The mast stepping and shroud plates were triangulated by thwarted struts and the tip of the mast appeared to be tickling the clouds.

We climbed aboard, noting the remarkable stability donated by the hard chines, and took a seat on a raised bench overhanging the gunwale while the Bermuda sails were run up and the boat was held carefully head to wind. Dick Wyche took the helm and we got a firm grip on the jib sheet. Then with a cautious push of the bow we left the pontoon and were off.

In the strong puffy breeze the boat dithered a moment and then dived for the lee bank like a hungry crocodile. With a thunder of flapping mainsail we put her about and roared across the river again. As I flattened out over the water with the jib sheet, I could see the sharp bow lifting nicely on its chine and could hear the water slashing past under the lee gunwale.

Two or three of these tremendous tacks and we bore away at ferocious speed to run upstream. This gave us a chance to catch our breath and the boat ran very steadily with the kicking strap controlling the huge sail and damping all tendency to roll. We felt the boat surge forward immediately in the puffs and there was an intriguing ridge or feather of water streaming from the pointed stern.

Once more we put her on the wind and had another five minutes of the wildest excitement it has ever been my lot to experience in a sailing boat and then we stepped ashore for a breather.

Dick Wyche stroked his pointed chin thoughtfully, looked at me and said, " Do you know ? I think that boat is capable of 18 knots ! " I don't disbelieve him, and one of the reasons for thinking so is that the weight of the new plywood hull is only 200lb.

**Justin Scott standing
beside *Scoter*.**

photo: Celia Scott

In 1953, Justin Scott's offer to buy *Scoter* for £200 was accepted.

The same year members built a new pontoon, fitted a starters box and equipped it with a modern galley. Henley Curl agreed that his brother's legacy could be used for the purpose and the pontoon was duly named *John Curl*. For the 1954 season, the club had a quarters for a race officer and catering facilities but no changing or toilet facilities. A raft was constructed on paint drums with a structure on top (alright; a shed) the £135 cost was nearly covered by member donations and the new raft was named *Kon Tiki*, after Thor Heyerdahl's exploits in the Pacific on a papyrus raft of the same name.

Another new punt was added to the fleet in 1954. *Martin* had failed to beat *Swallow II* and Basil and Kitty Tracey ordered a new plywood punt from Wyche & Coppock. Their third punt was to be called *Melanitta*.

right

Basil Tracey in what was to become typical pose sailing *Melanitta*.

photo: Peter Tracey

Andrew Anderson later commissioned this silver model of *Melanitta* from Peter Tillett.

photographed by courtesy of Andrew and Mrs. Jo. Anderson

In 1956, the club were again represented at the Olympic Games when Tim Whelpton attended as reserve for Star Class in Melbourne. Tim had won the Star class Olympic selection trials but as he'd skippered a yacht in the Mediterranean, there were doubts over his amateur status and Bruce Banks sailed in his place. Tim and his sister Evadne both owned Punts and their father E.P. Whelpton had owned *Pintail* for a couple of years after the war. In 1948 the family purchased *Curlew*, one of the one design punts. At the same time Tim's brother-in-law John Eastwood, part owned *Kipper*, another one design punt with his sister Eileen.

Tim Whelpton at the helm of *Honey Lam* leading *Starkasten*.

photo: Beken

That year, commodore Peter Standley was able to advise members of a remarkable turn around in the club's finances over the last five years - from a state of near bankruptcy to a position where reserves were being built up to replace the club's pontoons. Sailing clubs are either run for their members or by them and the club's change in fortune was very largely down to Dr Basil Tracey's efforts in maintaining the existing pontoons.

Swallow II

Gerald Sambrooke Sturgess crewed by Mike Stannard.

photo: Judy Macdonald (nee Sturgess) and Peter Sturgess

In 1956, the club purchased the moulds for the plywood punt from Wyche & Coppock for £20.00. Landamores of Wroxham built *Snark* for two farmers *Snow, Arnold and their kids*. The following year, Tom Harmer, then rear commodore, set about the immaculate construction of *Flamer* (later *Greylag*) with Norwich solicitor, Keith Flatman. Wyche and Coppock had only built two Norfolk Punts and Dick Wyche might have been surprised to learn the number of hulls that had been built to his design over fifty years.

It's difficult to imagine today the confusion that existed when individual clubs had their own racing rules - particularly in view of the significant common membership. Up to 1924, Horning Town Sailing Club had insisted that yachts with an overlap could not be luffed. As late as 1947, attempts to coordinate international racing rules foundered on vested interests and impatience when the Americans, not then members of the International Yacht Racing Union, introduced their own new rules. For the next ten years there were two conflicting rule books for international competition. Gerald Sambrooke Sturgess was by then an internationally acclaimed authority on yacht racing rules and pivotal in establishing the new international rules. Peter Scott was elected President of the International Yacht Racing Union in 1956 and said of Gerald: " I had often sailed against him in the old days on the Norfolk Broads. He has made himself the greatest expert on the wording and case law of both sets of rules." In 1957, the International Yacht Racing Union was able to establish the first, single set of International Racing Rules.

On one of his return visits to the Broads in 1958, Stewart Morris was invited to sail *Melanitta* and commented of the plywood punt: "Not only outstandingly fast but most sensitive with the feel of a thoroughbred. Yes indeed!" High praise from the maestro.

In the meantime, the Norfolk Punt Club was beginning to prosper and members felt sufficiently confident to raise subscriptions to £1. This was a period when racing Norfolk Punts was the sport of husbands and wives and whilst 'Terylene' sails were permitted in 1959, trapezes remained prohibited. Leslie Landamore of Wroxham built a batch of six wooden, replacement punt masts and Dr. Basil Tracey in "The Dinghy Yearbook" claimed the new spars were "based on Star class practice, as used by Lipincott in the US." He went on to elaborate: "Diamonds have been abandoned, breakages having been due to compression and the failure of one spreader. Of the 26ft of mast, 10ft is from the deck stepping to the crosstrees and the lower shrouds, 8ft more to the hounds and the top 8ft is unsupported. The width of the crosstrees is designed so the lower and upper shrouds are parallel, and have a large outward component for their downward compression on the mast. It is found that provided the lower shrouds are sufficiently taught, the mast takes an admirable controlled amount of bend. Throughout the season the masts have proved most reliable. The shrouds are placed two inches behind the mast step and the section of mast is $3\frac{1}{2}$" by $2\frac{1}{2}$"." He went on to remark that 176 square feet of sail was a lot to carry on a simply rigged mast.

In 1960 the Royal Geographic Society published a report written by Lambert, Jennings, Smith, Green and Hutchinson which turned conventional wisdom about the origin of the Broads on its head. Dr. Joyce Lambert had turned over two thousand test bores by hand and come to the conclusion that the Broads were flooded mediaeval peat diggings. The Victorians had believed the Broads were just peaty lagoons left by a retreating sea and scant thought had ever been given that the Broads may have been man made. Place names such as Barton Turf might have provided a clue and there had been a suggestion as early as 1834 from Samuel Woodward that Barton Broad "said to have been called the Deep Fen in the time of Edward III and may have become waters by the continued cutting of turf out of it...." Nevertheless, the conclusions drawn by Joyce Lambert and her team that the Broads were a man made landscape astonished her contemporaries.

There is little natural stone in this corner of East Anglia and wood had to be saved for building. Turf was cut, dried and burnt as a readily available fuel. Barton Broad had been dredged in 1949, when a large amount of reed swamp was removed from the east banks and the surrounding reed beds later became some of the worst affected by coypu. The FRGS team used an old aerial photograph of Barton Broad taken before the 1949 dredging to illustrate how the peat was cut:

photo: Aerofilms of Boreham Wood

To prevent flooding, turf was dug in sections leaving a solid wall of peat separating individual strips. Lines of demarcation, in this case the the Barton-Irstead boundary were left as wider baulks of undug peat which remain today as the island. These shallow 'peninsulas' grew vegetation more quickly and can be seen today on many Broads. This photograph clearly shows these 'peninsulas' and the different alignment of the Barton and Irstead parishes diggings. 'Clever' Catfield villagers had a public staithe and rights to dig turf on what became both Hickling and Barton Broads. Their Barton staithe enabled them to avoid paying tolls at Potter Heigham bridge!

The manor of Bartonbury Hall at Barton Turf had included three valuable fisheries in 1572. One was the river between Stalham and Barton and it seems that Barton Broad ("an area below Barton town") was divided into areas of fishing. Simon Tobyes is recorded as having three acres of fishing and two other areas were known as Buryallewater and Seyveswater and presumably corresponded to areas that were originally peat diggings. Both were rented out at eight shillings a year as early as 1415/1435, so Barton Broad must have been largely in existence by that date. These fifteenth century records also describe what we now know as Limekiln dyke up to Neatishead as a fishery called Burwodeswer. Most peat was excavated some distance away from the rivers to prevent flooding - which is why so many broads are found in side valleys and often connected to the main river by a short dyke. During the years of peat excavation this also applied to Barton Broad. The River Ant was diverted to flow through the flooded peat diggings, possibly to increase their value as a fishery. The original course of the Ant can be found to the east of the Broad and survives in part as a ditch marking the Barton - Catfield parish boundary.

The River Ant has undergone more alterations to its course than any river in the Broads system. Further downstream, there is evidence that a cut was dug across the causeway from St. Benets to St. John's hospital to create Ant Mouth. The lower Ant had previously skirted St. Benets along the Hundred dyke and flowed into the river Thurne. The Thurne then flowed in the opposite direction and emptied into the sea along Sock Drain. Travelling upstream on the Thurne towards West Somerton, Sock Drain is a straight dyke that leaves the main river at Dungeon Corner, beside Martham Broad. Where the Thurne flowed into the sea has become the weakest point in our sea defences. The current possibility of a permanent breach raises the rather alarming possibility that the River Thurne, if left to its own devices, may once again reverse its direction and flow directly into the sea.

Gerald Sambrooke Sturgess with *Swallow II* at Cox's yard at Barton Turf shortly before he sold her.

photo: courtesy Mike Evans

Billy de Quincey in *Wild Duck*.

photo: Jane de Quincey

After *Flamer*, there was a period of five years when no new punts were built until Eastwood Whelpton at Upton produced *Harnser* for John Plaice in 1961. *Wild Duck*, *Wild Goose* and *Tern* followed in swift succession. *Wild Duck* was originally owned by Billy de Quincey and partners, although he became sole owner within a couple of years. *Wild Goose* was another Tracey family punt and Angwin Eddy had *Tern*. His sons Peter and David, having cut their teeth in the Scorpion class, campaigned *Tern* very successfully for a number of years.

Wild Goose **under construction at Upton.**

photo: Peter Tracey

It would be foolish to try and describe Basil Tracey as anything other than eccentric. He was a kind man with wild, wind blown hair who possessed a fine voice, which he exercised at every opportunity.

Andrew Anderson recalled: "Basil's attitude to his fellow competitors, when it looked likely that a change in *Wild Goose's* direction was immediately necessary was based on Darwin's Theory of the survival of the fittest, or in his case, the Loudest. ie. If you generate enough nautical abuse you are bound to escape the looming carnage." His running commentary could be heard all round the course.

The good doctor had an inimitable sun hat and a massive pair of khaki shorts; whilst Kitty crewed the family punt wearing a tweed skirt. The pair kept a fearless wire haired terrier called Ginger and their motor cruiser *Elizabeth* served as tug and mother hen to most of the Norfolk Punt fleet. She towed the fleet to Hickling and Wroxham every year and most found welcome and a cup of tea on board and possibly a tow out to the Broad. At either end of the season, *Elizabeth* would tow *Melanitta* or *Wild Goose* to and from Clifford Allen's yard at Coltishall.

Tim Whelpton and Basil Tracey debate the finer points of a Proctor gooseneck before the launch of *Wild Goose*.

photo: Peter Tracey

left

Wild Goose being launched on a freezing day by Kitty Tracey.

right

Everyone was invited for a sail in the new punt as soon as she was launched.

photos: Peter Tracey

After the euphoria of a generation of new punts, mother nature had been to work on the club pontoons and the original structures due for replacement. Members working parties were organised under the careful eye of co-ordinator Tom Harmer.

Building a new pontoon. Standing at the rear are Angwin Eddy and Tom Harmer.

photo: Peter Tracey

Mooring the new WC and changing facility. Dr. Frank Tubbs is holding the post upright. Greshams School Sailing Club was affiliated with the Norfolk Punt Club and contributed half the cost of the 'shed.'

photo: Peter Tracey

June 12th 1965. Four NPC commodores raced *Swealtsje* in the Three Rivers Race.
left to right: Edward C. Pollit, Reggie Wylie, Roger Pollit, Justin Scott.

photo: Celia Scott

With a rush of new, lightweight and much more easily trailable punts, the class became significantly more adventurous. Several owners had friends and relations who sailed at Aldeburgh in Suffolk and the sheltered waters of the Alde suited Norfolk Punts well. Aldeburgh became a regular visit.

far left
Kingfisher at Aldeburgh.

left
Tom Carter.

photos: Tom Clarke

David Adler at Aldeburgh.

photo: Tom Clarke

'One of a Kind' boat-for-boat trials were very popular and the Norfolk Punt gained a Portsmouth Yardstick of 98 - establishing the plywood punts as the fastest single hulled class in the UK. This new found status began to attract attention from further afield. Jack Chippendale recalled fitting twin sliding seats to a Norfolk Punt to take part in a cross Channel race. One of Chippendale's directors, Mike Pruett was determined to take part and sailed as a three man crew with John Oakley and Cliff Norbury.

Wroxham Week 1968

There were fewer River Cruisers competing in Wroxham Week during the 1960s and the punts class shared the water for their lunchtime race.

Tom Harmer had very kindly lent *Kingfisher* to the Author for the week. A capsize around a gybe mark in close company with a cruiser ended in one of the more embarrassing moments in an extended yachting career.

photo: Authors collection

Gerald Sambrooke Sturgess and Peter Scott chatting before the International Yacht Racing Union AGM in 1968.

photo:
Judy Macdonald (nee Sturgess) and Peter Sturgess

Mike Evans leads away from the start of a Norfolk Punt race in *Rushlight* during Wroxham Week 1970.

photo: Eastern Daily Press

The mid 1970s saw a modest revival of Norfolk punt building, although the new boats were all amateur built. Even in plywood, the cost of a professionally built boat was rising swiftly. Derek Gibbs comes from a long line of Broadsmen. His grandfather, Charlie Gibbs had been responsible for keeping Surlingham Broad open to the public after a disagreement with a local landowner. The dispute was aided by a punt gun and settled over a bottle of scotch. In 1975, Derek built himself *Shoveller*.

Derek Gibbs in *Shoveller*, crewed by Robin Myhill.

photo: Derek Gibbs

The pair enjoyed some success and won the Cock of the Broads in 1977. This trophy was awarded to the fastest boat at Thurne Mouth Open Regatta. It is now a River Cruiser trophy.

photos: Derek Gibbs

Angwin Eddy crewed by son David in *Tern*, winning the local boats handicap race at Barton regatta in 1970.

photo: Jane de Quincey

David Adler, crewed by David Eddy in *Greylag*.

photo: courtesy Jane de Quincey

left

Basil Tracey crewed by Tony Faulkner in *Wild Goose*.

below

Hickling Regatta 1976.

photos: courtesy Jane de Quincey

In 1976, The Norfolk Punt Club celebrated its Golden Jubilee and saw the formation of the Fibreglass Norfolk Punts Fund Association. Club commodore, David Adler chaired the association, with co-trustees Tom Harmer and Justin Scott. Their object was to fund development of a new mould to build fibreglass Norfolk Punts. It was estimated that £2,500 would be required to make a mould and a prototype and a formal contract was drawn up between the association and builder, Colin McDougall. Derek Gibbs bravely volunteered *Shoveller* to be used as a plug. She escaped largely undamaged and after some realignment of the deck profile, the plug was ready.

The new association had certainly set itself a challenge and at times the project must have seemed fraught with difficulty. The moulders went into voluntary liquidation and when the first hull was produced and launched on 23rd July 1977, it weighed around a hundred pounds over the maximum weight specified. Her rudder broke twice in quick succession and Colin McDougall agreed to produce a second prototype to be delivered by August 19th, in time for the 1977 Norfolk Punt Championships and named appropriately *Golden Jubilee*.

Golden Jubilee's first sail. Derek Gibbs had rigged her and is trapezing whilst David Adler helms.

A group of keen punt sailors took *Golden Jubilee* to the John Player sponsored World Sailing Speed Record Week at Portland, held during the first week in October 1977. In less than ideal conditions *Golden Jubilee* achieved 13.8 knots. Wind speed at the time was recorded at 30 knots! At the same event, Sir Timothy Colman broke the world sailing speed record in *Crossbow*, with Tim Whelpton as part of his crew. Norfolk Punts received more publicity during this period than ever before or since.

Norfolk Punts

This is the photograph of *Golden Jubilee* at the 1977 World Sailing speed Record Week that was submitted to caption Julia Carter's article in Yachts and Yachting. David Adler is at the helm with Colin McDougall.

Julia Carter won the class a two page spread on Norfolk Punts in Yachts and Yachting. *Golden Jubilee* was taken to the London Dinghy Exhibition. Hugh Wylam and David Blackburne sailed her in the Burnham Icicle and she was taken as far away as Rutland, Queen Mary reservoir at Staines, Brancaster, Conniston, Aldeburgh ....

The class rules required alteration to permit glass fibre construction but on her return from Portland, Jack Chippendale measured *Golden Jubilee* and reported that she had insufficient rocker. Despite considerable publicity, orders for new boats were slow to materialise and an out-of-control sailing cruiser inflicted some serious damage to *Golden Jubilee's* deck at Thurne Mouth. It was decided to repair the deck and sell the boat. Orders started to trickle and Colin McDougall produced *Swallowtail, Marsh Harrier and Grebe*. The boats weren't without teething problems which, whilst they will have been expensive to the builder, formed an essential part of a learning curve. The flat surfaces and sharp corners that Dick Wyche had drawn nearly a quarter of a century earlier, were just right for plywood but all of the ply classes designed in the fifties and sixties, struggled with transition to glassfibre construction. Their flat surfaces flexed and sharp edges chipped and broke away easily. Maintaining panel stiffness often proved more expensive than moulding a round shape - and the plywood Norfolk Punt had larger flat areas and sharper corners than most. Flexible panels also gave considerable problems maintaining the seal of built-in buoyancy tanks to the hull.

The fleet continued to travel. *Avocet* on Lake Conniston in 1978.

photo: Celia Scott

In 1979 it was *Swallowtail's* turn for an epic voyage. Colin and Duncan McDougall sailed her from Ranworth dam to Brancaster. They managed to get a tow down the Bure on Saturday, on Sunday night pulled her up the beach at Sheringham and arrived at Brancaster on Monday. The trip was made in generally light weather but was not without incident. A main shroud became detached from its spreader off the North Norfolk coast and a member of the public summoned the Police in Great Yarmouth when they saw an unmanned punt beside Haven Bridge and feared the crew might have drowned.

Firefly.

photo: Chris Tovell

The well travelled *Avocet* on the Thames at Greenwich.

photo: Celia Scott

In 1980, a varied team of six Norfolk Punts, ranging from *Rosybill* to *Golden Jubilee* raced on the Thames at Greenwich against a team of 18 foot skiffs. Both these punts were unfortunate to lose their masts in strong winds of the Sunday racing. *Avocet, Golden Jubilee, Greylag, Harnser, Kingfisher, Puffin* and *Rosybill* failed to beat the skiffs but all agreed it was a worthwhile experience and the first time a fleet of Norfolk Punts had raced beside Tower Bridge.

By 1982, the Fibreglass Norfolk Punts Fund Association had been in existence for five years. By then only four fibreglass and two composite punts had been built from the mould and the Association was wound up. Loans were paid off but twenty five equity members received twenty pence for each pound contributed and the moulds were passed to the Norfolk Punt Club.

A start at the 1982 Norfolk Punt National Championships.

photo: Richard Sadler

A light weather spinnaker run in 1982. Probably unexciting sailing but the photograph illustrates the extent of punt spinnaker development at the time.

photo: Richard Sadler

John Findlay, mine host of the Fisherman's Return Inn at Winterton and an enthusiast of traditional punts (and one of a growing band that have felt obliged to own several Norfolk Punts simultaneously), approached Andrew Wolstenholme to design him a new, traditional Norfolk Punt. Andrew was advised by the Class Secretary, Richard Sadler, that a traditional Norfolk Punt would no longer be acceptable under the class rules, but a double chine punt would be approved. The class could see advantages in the twin chine construction of *Reedham Nan* and the possibility of producing low cost kits for easy home construction. Andrew had already designed a 'stitch and glue', double-chine rowing skiff *Sprite* and both he and John felt that they could produce a punt which might give the class a boost without necessarily rendering existing punts obsolete. The problem was that the double chine design didn't fit the class rules. Andrew drew what he describes as a conservative hull shape and *Reedham Nan* was built by Fred Saunders. The punt was named after John's late grandmother from Reedham who had left him the money for the new boat! During discussions at various meetings, on how to make room for the new design within class rules, Tom Harmer suggested reversion to the pre-war class rules that permitted a wide variety of hull construction.

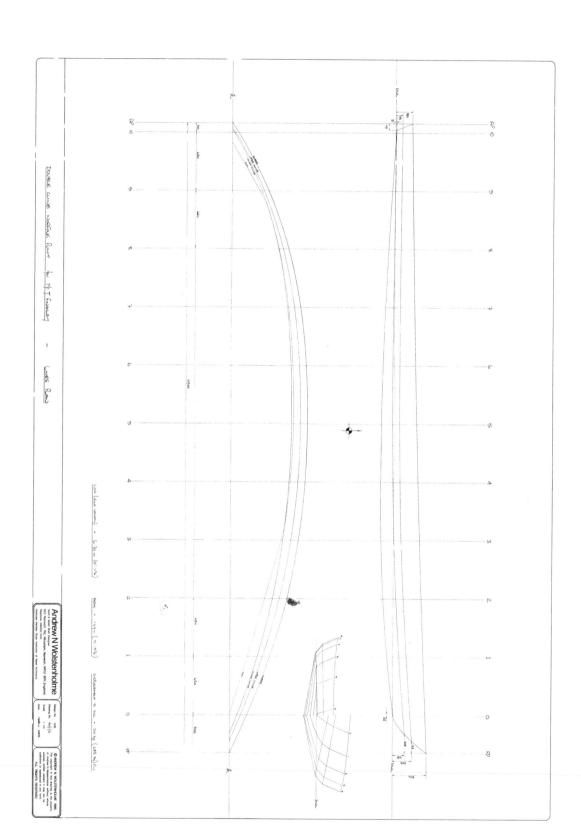

Lines of punt 73 *Reedham Nan* supplied and reproduced by courtesy of Andrew Wolstenholme

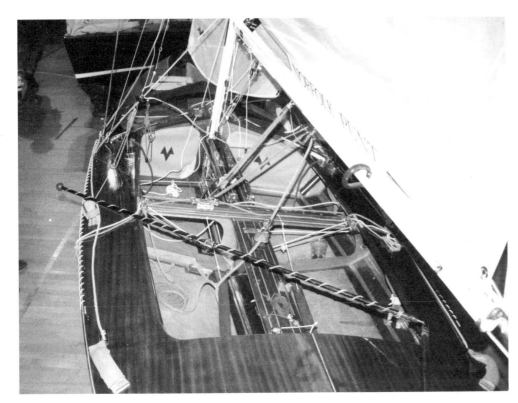

Crystal Palace.

photo: James Hoseason

The class continued to exhibit at London Dinghy Exhibitions and in 1985, *Reedham Nan* was trailed to Crystal Palace. The rest of the fleet went about their business as if nothing could disturb their calm.

Class Secretary Richard Sadler with Sarah Williams on board *Reed Bunting.*

photo: Richard Sadler

Start of a race in the mid 1980s.

photo: Richard Sadler

James Sadler and Tim Jacob push *Decoy* down a windy reach during the 1986 class championships.

photo: Richard Sadler

Punts had used a single trapeze since the early 1960s, largely as a result of their visits to Aldeburgh. Initially they were only used in allcomers racing at Barton. The finer points of work on the wire did not always seem so straightforward!

photo: Richard Sadler

far left

The starters hut at Barton.
photo: James Hoseason

left

Simon Read in *Curlew*.
photo: Richard Sadler

James Hoseason and Warwick Woodall on a three sail reach in *Razorbill* **during the 1989 Bloody Mary race at Queen Mary reservoir at Staines in West London.**

photo: James Hoseason

Chapter Four
Revolution

Removing the restrictions on methods of construction to permit *Reedham Nan* in the class had wider implications than was possibly realised at the time. No-one came forward to produce kit boats to the *Reedham Nan* design and she remains the only double chine punt built. In some respects this was a pity. When considered beside subsequent hull shapes, she hadn't been drawn on a level playing field and in different circumstances might have made a major contribution to the class.

Neal Duffield and Rick Sargeant sailing *Razorbill* on the Thurne.

photo: Tricia Duffield

Andrew Wolstenholme and John Findlay had done little more than spend their time and money trying to help the class move forward in what seemed a sensible direction at the time. This was the end of their involvement with racing punts. John subsequently asked Andrew to produce a short punt for him that could never comply with class rules. Maynard Watson built the new boat that was christened *Esox*. Brothers of the angle will have already spotted a pike in the water.

Nevertheless, the floodgates had been thrown wide open for unlimited development and in 1988, the class witnessed the launch of one of the most radical design changes ever. Class Secretary Richard Sadler asked Phil Morrison to design him a Norfolk Punt to take full advantage of the new rules.

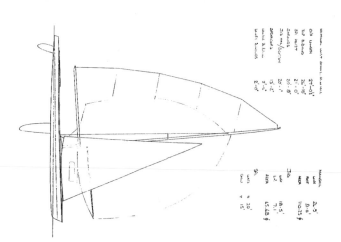

Drawings reproduced by courtesy of Phil Morrison.

Phil Morrison is a modest, self-effacing man with a large number of highly successful designs to his credit, ranging from restricted class dinghies right through to short-handed offshore, mono and multihulls. When questioned about his Norfolk Punt design he remarked that he was told to "do his damnedest" and went on to comment that he'd just done his thing and that naval architects are said to have only one design in them and his was the *China Doll* design of National 12! When pressed, he recalled "at the time Richard Sadler advised me that the class were considering twin trapezes and possibly some more sailing on open water, so I designed her with that in mind. Twin trapezes were accepted at the 1986 AGM and *Blackbird* set the scene for a burst of unprecedented change and development. She was beautifully built by Simon Reed and launched in 1988. The Morrison design had much wider stern sections than either the Wyche & Coppock hull or the double chine punt. Double-ended sailing boats have a tendency to drag their sterns at speed and the heavily veed bows of the Wyche & Coppock design unusually required crew weight to move for'ard to maintain optimum planing. The Morrison hulls were indeed quick in a blow but the additional wetted surface area of their wider sterns made them slower than the old hard chine design in light weather. Nevertheless, the class had leapt from what barely qualified as a restricted class to out-and-out unrestricted development.

Blackbird in Chichester Harbour.

photo: Richard Sadler

Blackbird. Deck view.

photo: James Hoseason

Matthew Thwaites in
Rainbow Trout.

**1989 PUNT
CHAMPIONSHIPS**

photos: James Hoseason

Fred and George.

**Tom and Richard Clarke
in** *Kipper.*

photo: James Hoseason

The new rules provided an opportunity to update some of the older punts.

left
Kingfisher.

below right
Harnser.

photos: Chris Tovell

far left

Whilst some owners were renovating older punts, others were determined to squeeze all they could from the new design. *Swift* featured a transom hung rudder.

photo: Richard Parker

right
Rhode Island Red under construction, showing off her carbon fibre credentials and cockpit drain tubes.

far right
Matthew Thwaites working on the boat.

photos: James Hoseason

In 1989 the class accepted James Hoseason's proposals that fully battened mainsails and sails made from non-woven cloths such as Mylar be permitted. This was a sensible alteration as these sails are able to remain competitive for longer and less inclined to pull out of shape when righting after a capsize with possibly a ton of water laying in them - even if they aren't quite as pretty.

Gerald Sambrooke Sturgess.
photo: Judy Macdonald (nee Sturgess and Peter Sturgess)

Stewart Morris.
photo: Thomas Vaughan

1991 saw the club lose a whole generation of its most senior members. Dr. Basil Tracey died aged 91. Basil's first punt was *Rushlight* which he took over from his brother-in-law in 1936. He not only enjoyed his sailing but put a great deal of hard work and effort into the club; not to mention public spirited generosity in ordering new punts when the class needed a boost. He had been the driving force behind the club's revival after the war and continued to take great interest in the clubs affairs. At the age of 90, he set out with his son Peter in *Melanitta* (which he had repurchased) and capsized in full view of the pontoon. Basil emerged damp but still smiling.

Gerald Sambrooke Sturgess, the last surviving founder member of the Norfolk Punt Club died at his home at Barton Turf in August of the same year after a short illness, aged 89. *Swallow II*, which he owned with his father in law, had been seminal to the class for nearly fifty years. He served as commodore of the Yare & Bure Sailing Club in 1936; commodore of the Norfolk Punt Club from 1938 - 1946, again in 1950, and commodore of the Norfolk Broads Yacht Club in 1948. He was also a committee member of the Royal Norfolk & Suffolk Yacht Club for many years after the war and rear commodore of that club in 1974 and 1975. His contribution to international yacht racing was formally recognised by the Order of the British Empire in 1983.

Stewart Morris died in 1991, aged 81. Since the death of his father in 1935, he had largely ceased to compete on the Broads and lived at Itchenor, beside Chichester harbour. He was a regular visitor and never lost touch with his roots in Norfolk Punts. Many local sailing clubs found themselves unexpected beneficiaries of his will.

Justin Scott's sisters acquired *Titmouse (Swallow I)* in 1936 and Justin and his brother Gavin used to camp in her before the war. His first punt was *Sandpiper*, which he restored and he sailed with Tom Harmer from from Thorpe to Acle. She was followed by *Scoter* the first plywood punt and lastly *Avocet*.

Billy de Quincey was an extremely experienced yachtsman with a very successful family pedigree in the sport. His father had been commodore of the Royal Canoe Club and his brother Roger had partnered Uffa Fox in their successful International Canoe challenges against the Americans during the 1930s. Billy himself was part of the successful International Fourteen teams of the 1930s and was a member of the amateur crew shipped on board *Endeavour* for her Americas Cup Challenge. His ownership of Norfolk Punts started in 1961 and he retained *Wild Goose* until 1979.

All five men had been involved with Norfolk Punts for many years and their loss in a single year was a considerable blow.

In 1991 Mike Evans discovered *Shrimp*, the first Norfolk Punt to be registered in the class, lying at the Norfolk Education Committee Sailing Centre at Filby. Her rig was missing but by referring to Gerald Sambrooke Sturgess' records, Michael decided she must have originally carried a simple lug rig. He found some old spars with an authentic look about them; Jeckells cut down an old, cotton Yare & Bure mainsail to fit and *Shrimp* travelled to Greenwich. In a letter to Hugh Tusting dated 2nd February 1982, Stewart Morris recalled in his tiny, almost indecipherable hand: "*Shrimp* was built by Walter Woods in the winter of 1917/18 (for quanting) After the war, she was given a centreboard case and a case aft for insertion of a rudder and a small triangular sail laced to the mast - boom and spar put into sockets at tack and clew - and was my boat. I used to paddle her to windward in Meadow dyke when going from Hickling to Horsey and put up the sail (and insert the rudder) when in open water - or the wind freed. 16' long she got a good handicap, for racing had a sloop rig - 1924 onwards."

Shrimp, presented to the National Maritime Museum at Greenwich. June 2nd 1994.
l to r
David Skinner, Tom Clarke and Michael Evans.

photo: Tom Clarke

Shrimp, displayed at the National Maritime Museum at Falmouth.

photo: courtesy National Maritime Museum.

The Greenwich Museum has a fine history with commercial sail but has traditionally struggled with 'leisure' craft. When the Queen opened the new £28m, National Maritime Museum at Falmouth on the 14th March 2003, old *Shrimp* headed west. She is on public display and currently hanging from their ceiling. This provides an unusual view of a small boat and Cornwall may not be the most convenient location for a Norfolk Punt enthusiast to inspect the first boat registered in the class but she is at least safe and sound.

Richard Parker and James Gill sailing Shag.

photo: Anna Gill

Preparatory signal.

photo: Chris Tovell

A surprising side effect of narrowing the market for racing Norfolk Punts has been a growth in enthusiasm for older punts. The athletic requirements of the new designs have caused enthusiasts to widen the class in search of a more restrained sail and several, more traditional designs have been produced. With this has come the realisation that Norfolk Punts have a wide variety of leisure uses and don't have to be solely 'machines for racing.'

Mike Evans crewed by Edward Whipp at full chat in *Swallow II*.

*photo:
Eastern Daily Press*

right
Arthur Thain in
Stickleback **and**
far right
Limelight **in 1999.**

photos: Chris Tovell

Decoy.
Percy's handiwork still
going strong in 1999.

photo: Chris Tovell

Gamecock **in Paul Bown's**
workshop being rebuilt for
the Rev. Neville
Khambatta.

photo: James Hoseason

Fabian Bush produced *Scoot* and *Goosander* and built both to a very high standard of finish.

Two shots of Marion Bown with *Goosander* taken by Chris Tovell.

1995 saw the launch of the first Norfolk Punt designed by Stephen Jones. *Cuckoo* was again beautifully crafted by Essex boatbuilder Fabian Bush, on this occasion for Peter Bainbridge. Suddenly, there was a resurgence of punts with clinker topsides, for no obvious reason beyond personal preference.

Fabian Bush fitting the hog near *Cuckoo's* bow.

photo: Peter Bainbridge

Cuckoo at Plain Sailing in Wroxham for rigging.

photos: Author

The Norfolk Punt Club logo is a brilliant piece of graphics. The design recently 'grew' an extended roach to its mainsail but few today realise the simple graphics first saw the light of day as the front cover of the 1936 Norfolk Punt Club handbook. Admirers have found an ever extending series of uses for the logo which has become a silent ambassador for the class.

left

Anne Evans's brooch.

far left

Celia Scott's weather vane.

photos: Author

**Punt Championships
c. 1990.**

photo: Chris Tovell

By the mid 1990s, algal bloom had rendered Barton virtually a sterile water as nature had been working away at turning the Broad back into peat bogs. Deposition over the last forty years had equalled the amount of silting over the last four hundred. The 'Clearwater 2000' scheme not only provided opportunities for biomanipulation but the multi million pound dredging scheme that removed 300,000 cubic metres of sediment has made Barton the finest sailing water on the Broads.

Peregrine.

photo: Richard Parker

Merlin.

photo: Roger Taylor

Saker.

photo: Anna Gill

Peter Bainbridge has a long and successful history in international racing and in 2000 replaced *Cuckoo* with *Whooper,* another Stephen Jones design. She was to carry a modern rig, be built down to weight and measure at twenty two feet overall. The new punt has proved a happy middle course in all weather conditions, able to compete equally against the hard chine boats in light weather and the Morrisons in a blow.

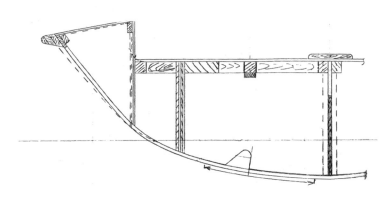

Stephen Jones drew easy curves for *Whooper's* sections.

**right
Section 8.**

**far right
Section 5.**

reproduced by courtesy of Stephen Jones

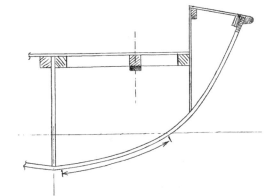

Ben Bainbridge visits Richard Faulkner's yard at Hamble during the construction of *Whooper.*

photo: Peter Bainbridge

Norfolk Punts have regularly been successful in Horning Sailing Club's Three Rivers Race. This race involves rounding marks usually placed at Ludham, South Walsham, Hickling and on the lower Bure, usually somewhere near the Stracey Arms. Skippers are permitted to take the marks in any order to take best advantage of wind and tide. The race starts earlier now than it used to but the event is usually sailed on the first weekend in June to coincide with a full moon. Punts have regularly been first to finish this race, which at least permits more sleep than other competitors!

Richard Parker helps James Hoseason into his harness for the 1989 Three Rivers Race in *Razorbill.*

photo: James Hoseason

Peter Bainbridge, crewed by elder son Alex, gained a measure of revenge for his second place in the inaugural Three Rivers Race when he won the event in *Whooper* in 2001.

Peter and Alex Bainbridge in *Whooper* **for the Three Rivers Race. The photograph illustrates her original deck layout.**

photo: Nick Mockridge

The classes appetite for development has continued unabated and whilst Richard Parker of Boats and Bits in Norwich was busy developing the Morrison hulls, his father John decided that down-to-weight glass hulls built to the Wyche and Coppock design were the way to go. The project grew out of discussions after Wednesday evening racing at Hickling and John's first glass hull *Snowgoose*, built from the class moulds saw the water in the spring of 2003.

right and far right

***Snowgoose* decked and fitting out ....**

photos: Jane Pye

.... and launched.

Jeff Green's hull
mouldings look
straightforward enough ....

photo: Jane Pye

.... until James Jarvey
starts to fit the woodwork.
This is Chris Woods'
Woodpecker ready for her
decks.

photo: Jane Pye

Nicky Barker seems to be enjoying herself on _Snowgoose's_ trapeze during the 2003 Championships.

photo: Rachel Clayton

The class accepted both asymmetric spinakers and bowsprits. The asymmetrics gradually worked their way up the mast until they reached the masthead. The sails are a gift for photographers but rather better for speed than visibility!

Chris and Tash Pilling in _Blackbird_

photo: Rachel Clayton

Masthead asymmetrics in action.

photos: Rachel Clayton

Tom Virden and Robert Snelling at speed in *Saker*.

photo: Anna Gill

Hickling.

photos: Rachel Clayton

Hickling has always been a spiritual home for Norfolk Punts and Hickling Broad Sailing Club is now home to the largest fleet of Norfolk Punts.

In parallel and as if to prove the wider appeal of a Norfolk Punt, Andrew Anderson commissioned Andrew Wolstenholme to design an eighteen foot punt for sailing and rowing that he could use near his new Yorkshire home.

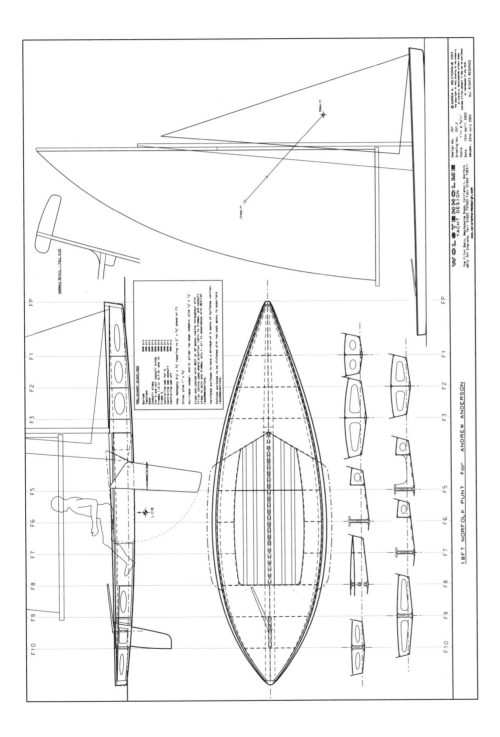

Reproduced by kind permission of Andrews Wolstenholme and Anderson.

Simon Girling and John Friend in *Cormorant*.

photo: Anna Gill

Championship start.

photo: Anna Gill

Punt Championships 2004.

photo: Chris Tovell

Saker.

photo: Anna Gill

After sixty years, the Norfolk Punt class is more successful today than at any time in its history. More Norfolk Punts of all persuasions have been built in recent years than ever before and turnouts for Norfolk Punt races are the highest in the classes history. Congratulations!

> *So point her up and haul your wind, get ready for the gun*
> *But never set your spinnaker until you're on the run.*
> *Though some may ride and some may shoot, while others like to hunt*
> *The finest sport in all the world is sailing in a punt.*

Eric Chamberlin. 1936.

Appendices
Norfolk Punt Club - Commodores

1927-30.	H.A.Morris	1993.	P.C.Watson
1930- 36.	Byron V.Noel	1994.	D.D.Skinner
1937-38.	A.L.Russell	1995.	M.Morrison
1938 -39.	G.Sambrooke Sturgess	1996.	Dr. R.Farman
1945-46.	G.Sambrooke Sturgess	1997.	J.S.Richards
1946-47.	Dr. B.M.Tracey	1998.	D.H.Adler
1947-49.	P.H.Cator	1999.	J.Friend
1949-50.	G.Sambrooke Sturgess	2000.	Miss. L.Levine
1950-51.	F.P.Standley	2001.	T.Scott
1951-53.	Col.D.Scott	2002.	S.Girling
1954.	C.R.Pollit	2003.	N.J.Dixey
1955.	P.H.Simon	2004.	William Glover
1956.	F.P.Standley	2005.	Mrs. Val. Khambatta
1957-58.	Dr. J.A.Eddy	2006.	Philip Dring
1959.	J.H.Scott		
1960-61.	T.E.Harmer		
1962.	Dr .B.M.Tracey		
1963.	R.McDonald Cobb		
1964-65.	W.B.de Quincey		
1966.	T.E.Carter		
1967.	Dr. A.H.C.Crouch		
1968.	E.C.Pollit		
1969-70.	T.H.Clarke		
1971-72.	E.H.Bradshaw		
1973-74.	J.H.Scott		
1975.	W.B.de Quincey		
1976-77.	D.H.Adler		
1978-79.	J.R.C.Wiley		
1980-81.	T.E.Carter		
1982.	Dr. R.U.Carr		
1983.	Dr. P.D.Knights		
1984-85.	E.H.Bradshaw		
1986-87.	J.D.Sennitt		
1988-89.	S.G.Daniels		
1900.	Dr. P.F.Roberts		
1991.	W.I.Rhodes		
1992.	C.R.D.McDougall		

Norfolk Punt Register

Considerable effort has been taken to ensure this register is accurate but between the passage of time and contradictions between sources, some inaccuracies are inevitable. If this proves to be the case, perhaps corrected details could be passed to the Class Secretary to update his records.

Unregistered early punts.

Hetebe.	1925.	W.F.Jermy, J.ff.Edge LOA 22' (described by Stewart Morris as "a proper gun punt")
Gannett.	1927.	M.J.Starling & W.Britten LOA. 18'
Neewyn.	1927.	H.W.Crotch
Athene.	1928.	Byron V. Noel
Dawn.	1928.	H.T.Percival
Red Quill.	1929.	Henley Curl
Scoter.	see class number 25	

1 *Shrimp.* 1917. Designer & builder: Walter Woods, Potter Heigham. LOA.17'
Owners:
1917.	H.A.Morris
1932.	C.Boardman
1958/69.	M.R.Boardman
1972/3.	Norfolk Education Committee
1991.	J.M.Evans
1994.	Presented to the National Maritime Museum (now at Falmouth)

Also registered as number 1 in the class: -
1 *Blue Winged Olive.* Designer & builder: Arthur Batchelor. LOA. 20'
Owners:
1936.   Arthur R. Batchelor
Hugh Wylam remembers as a young man seeing *BWO* rotting in the corner of the family garden at Witton Rectory, near Blofield.

2 *Jenny Spinner* 1927. Designer & builder: R.Southgate, Horning. LOA.19'
Owners:
1927/32..   A.R.Batchelor

3 *Bittern* 1929. Designer & builder: A.E.Pegg, Wroxham. LOA.19'8½"
Owners:
1929/50.   Lt.Cdr. S.A.Brooks RN

4 *Venture* 1925. Designer & builder: W.F.Jermy. LOA.22'
Owners:
1925.	W.F.Jermy
1930-38.	H.F.Webster

5 *Scud* 1927. Designer & builder: W.E.Mollett, 32 Bishopgate, Norwich. LOA.18'
Owners:
1927.	H.Bolingbroke
1938.	E.A.Ellis

Letter from Ted Ellis in 1968 described her as "an unusable hulk."

6 *Reed Pheasant* June 1927. Previous names: *Swallow, Titmouse.* Designer & Builder: W.G.Woods, Potter Heigham. LOA. 19'9"
Owners:
1927/36.   A.T.Chittock
1936/47.   Misses A.&.M.Scott (renamed *Titmouse*)
1947/73.   A.F.Savory (renamed *Reed Pheasant*)

7 *Pochard* 1909. Previous name: *Challenge.* "Built from Col. Hawkers measurements." Builders: Newstead & Woods, Cantley. LOA. 22'
Owners:
1909.   Lord Lucas
19 /72.   Lord Desborough KG, GCVO
1972.   Lt.Col. R.Sankey
31.10.72. Letter from G.S.Sturgess: "She has been lying under a tarpaulin on the bank at Whiteslea since before World War II and was in a pretty poor state of repair when I saw her during the summer. Col. Sankey wants to refit or reconstruct her." Colin McDougall advised that her rig and sails were in good condition at the time.

8 *Trout* 1926. Designer & builder: Walter Woods Potter, Heigham. LOA. 20'
Owners:
1926/32.   G.E.Morris
                   George Bishop (assistant warden at Whiteslea)
1990/95.   R.P.Groves
1999.   S.Bracey

9 *Sawbill* 1928. Designer & builder: Walter Woods, Potter Heigham. LOA. 19'
Owners:
1927/32.   Arnold Churchill

10 *Lapwing* 1928. previous name: *Mallard.* LOA. 18'
Owners:
1929/32.   Roland Wigg
1972/5.   A.Wright (renamed *Lapwing*)
1975.   Tom Appleton
1976.   Ian Miller. (purchased at Wroxham Boat Sale)
                   P.E.Martin

11 *Hickey* 1930. Designer & builder: C.E.Howard. LOA. 20'
Owners:
1932.   C.E.Howard
194   Ivan Sharp
Hickey has never raced.

12 *Smee* 1929. Designer & builder: unknown. LOA. 19'
Owners:
1932/5.   C.R.Howlett
1935.   F.&I.Green & D.Fisher
1936/38.   I.Green & D.Fisher
1938/47.   F. & I.Green
1947/52.   K.Green
1958/73.   W.J.Meek

13 *Swift* 1928. Designer & builder: Walter Woods, Potter Heigham. LOA. 20'
Owners:
1928/32.   Evelyn Shaw

14 *Pintail* 1929. Designer & builder: W.F.Jermy LOA. 19'8½"
Owners:
1929/36.   W.F.Jermy
1936/7.   Dr. & Mrs B.M.Tracey
1938/47.   P.P.Andrews & J.O.M.Wedderburn
1947/8.   E.P.Whelpton
1949/89.   W.P.E.Lake
1989.   Dr. Martin Scurr

15 *Tadpole.* 1930
Owners:
1930/2.   J.V.Cook

16 *Snipe* 1929. Previous name: *Harrier.* Designer & builder: H.C.Banham, Horning. LOA. 19'
Owners:
1929/31.   H.C.Crotch
1931/32.   Lord Albermarle
1932/36.   H.D.Harrison
1938/56.   Hugh Bainbridge
1956/69.   P.G.Leighton
1959.   - Cook (renamed *Snipe*)

17 *Stickleback* 1929. Designer & builder: Peter Arnold. LOA. 20'
Owners:
1929/56.   Peter Arnold
1956/69.   - Ling
1992.   A.G.Thaine

18 *Privateer* 1929. Previous name: *Winkle (1969).* Designer & builder: Dick Southgate, Horning. LOA. 19'
Owners:
1932/8.   Byron V. Noel
1947.   A.E.Burrell
1958/63.   12th Lowestoft Sea Scouts
1969.   J.W.K.Withers (renamed *Privateer*)
1986.   S.Bracey.
1995.   advised disintegrated

19 *Prawn* 1918. Designer: Walter Woods. Builder: Norfolk Broads Yachting Co., Potter Heigham. LOA.19'9"
Owners:
1918/36.   H.A.Morris
1936/52.   Dr. D.Mallam
1952/69.   B.G.Tusting
1999.   P.G.Tusting

20 *Stint* 1929. Designed & built by Uffa Fox, Cowes. LOA. 16'
Owners:
1929   Sir Edward Stracey. Bart.

21 *Flight* 1929. Designer & builder: Herbert Woods, Potter Heigham. LOA. 19'9"
Owners:
1929.	Herbert Woods
1930/37.	G.L.Fitt
1937/39.	Herbert Woods
1939/52.	S.F.Laws
1952/6	G.Loudon
196	S.Carter
1969/71.	C.Mann
1971/2002.	H.G.Tusting
2002.	P.Bown

22 *Scoulton Cob* 1929. Designer & builder: C.J.Broom, Brundall. LOA. 19'2"
Owners:
1929/32.	C.S.Robinson. Mid., RN

23 *Sparkle* 1930. Designer & builder: Dr. Boreham Trent. LOA. 20'
Owners:
1930/2.	T.H.Gordon Wright

24 *Heron* 1930. Designer & builder: Eric Chamberlin. LOA. 20'
Owners:
1930/3.	E.J.A.Chamberlin
1933/46.	D.A.G.Reid
	Mrs. R.Walker
1966.	E.Mills

25 *Snipe* 1930. Designer & builder: C.A.Grimes LOA. 19'9"
Owners:
1932/8.	A.J.&C.A.Grimes

Snipe is believed to have been destroyed in 1967.

Number reallocated in 1967 to *Goldeneye* 1929. previous name *Scoter*. Designed by George F.Marshall. Built by C.J.Broom, Brundall. LOA. 19'8"
1928.	W. Guy Daynes
1967/94.	E.C.Alston (name changed to *Goldeneye*)
2004.	Rev. Neville Khambatta

Scoter first raced unmeasured in 1934. *Goldeneye* was extensively rebuilt by Paul Bown in 2005.

26 *Spotlight* 1931. Designer & builder: Herbert Woods. LOA. 22'
Owners:
1931.	Herbert Woods
1969/85.	Mander College, Bedford
1985.	W.J.Linell

27 *Rushlight* 1930. Designer & builder: Herbert Woods. LOA. 21'11"
Owners:
1930.	H.G.Woods
1931/34.	F.J.Andrews
1934/36.	Tom Scott
1936/47.	Dr.&Mrs.B.M.Tracey
1947/67.	F.Peter Standley

1967/9.   J.O.Campbell, I.L.Smith & A.J.E.Landamore
1969/72..   J.M.Evans, J.Evans & B.Knox
19725.   Mr. & Mrs.D.C.B.Riviere
1975/77.   T.C.Earls
1977/81.   Mr.&Mrs.J.Williams
1987/9.   N.Birch & A. Donaldson
1989/96.   J.M.Evans
1996.   Mrs. C.Dixey

28 *Shuck* 1931. Designer & builder: T.F.Mase & W.E.Mollett. LOA. 20'
Owners:
1931/36.   T.F.Mase
1936/66.   G.K.Snow & C.B.Arnold
1966/82..   C.B.Arnold
1982/91.   Dr. J.R.Pilling
1991/92..   P.A.Luke
1992/97.   J.Richards & F. Trappes Lomax
1997/00.   A.Tibbenham
2000.   Pip Roney

29 *Stannicle* 1933. Designer & builder: Eric Chamberlin. LOA. 21' $9_{1/2}$"
Owners:
1933/50.   E.J.A.Chamberlin
1950/53.   Mr. & Mrs.R.W.Ormerod
1953/59.   A.W.May
1959/67.   P.A.Bastow
1967/73.   J.Harradine
1973/76.   A.Kirkpatrick
1976.   S.F.Read

30 *Dodman* 1933. Designer & builder: Herbert Woods. LOA. 21' 11"
Owners:
1933/70.   A.K.&C.Forbes
1970/72..   R.Webb
1972/90.   R.Fagin
1990.   C.M.Crawshaw (under restoration)

31 *Mickey* 1933. Designer & builder: Herbert Woods. LOA. 22'
Owners:
1933.   Martin Hodson
Martin Hodson took *Mickey* with him when he moved to Scotland.

32 *Cavender* 1933. Designer & builder: William Mollett. LOA. 21' 11"
Owners:
1933/35.   Capt. S.G.Wheeler
1935/39.   A.L.Russell
1939/47.   T.G.Gibb
1947/59.   G.T.Nunn
1959/65.   J.R.Howes
1965/86.   A.W.N.Eade. Mrs. J.Eade & A.J.Eade
1986/99.   R.Johnstone
1999.   T.Hubbard

33 *Sardine* 1934. Designer & builder: Herbert Woods. LOA. 22'
Owners:
1935/59.	Capt. C.B.Wilson MC
1959/63.	D.Roach
1963/72..	M.R.Stubbs
1972/9.	R&S.J.Smith
1979/83.	C.Chapman
1983/87.	D.Laws
1987/89.	A.Donaldson & N.Birch
1989/90.	J.M.Evans
1990.	Raymond Crisp

34 *Blue Dar* 1934. Designer & builder: W.E.Mollett. LOA. 22'
Owners:
1934/36.	E.N.Adcock
1936/66.	Mr.H.&Miss Cicely Bolingbroke
1969.	P.Bacon

35 *Swallow II* 1935 Designer & builder: Herbert Woods. LOA. 22'
Owners:
1935/60.	A.T.Chittock & G.S.Sturgess
1960/67.	Lt.Col.M.R.Braithwaite
1967/70.	T.S.M.Daniels.
1970/79.	T.W.Moore
1979/82.	S.Cooper & W.Clarke
1982/2001.	J.M.Evans
2001.	W.Daniels

36 *Rosybill* 1936 Previous names: *Ariel, Woodpecker.* Designer & builder: W.F.Jermy, Brundall. LOA. 22'
Owners:
1936.	W.F.Jermy
1936/8.	Dr.F.G.Maitland & Peter G.Beard
1939/47.	P.G.Beard & J.O.M.Wedderburn
1947/8.	Lt.Bruce H.Walker (renamed *Ariel*)
1948/56.	Col. D.Scott CBE, MC (renamed *Woodpecker* for the year.)
1949.	(renamed *Rosybill*)
1956/62.	R.Brown
1962/70.	Dr. F.R.Tubbs
1970/86.	J.R.C.Wiley
1986/99.	M.Morrison
1999.	M.Gibb

37 *Gamecock* 1936. Designer & builder: H.T.Percival, Horning. LOA. 22'
Owners:
1936/67.	Mr.& Mrs.Peter Cator
1967/70.	Dr. D.G.Wickner
1970/78.	Dr. I.M.M.Fraser
1978/85.	Mr.&Mrs.S.Barham
1985.	J.M.Evans
1986/9.	Paul Hinton
1989.	Rev & Mrs. N.Khambatta

38 *Sandpiper* 1936. previous name: *Sprat* Designer & builder: John S.Neal. LOA. 22′
Owners:
1936/49.	John S.Neal
1949/54.	J.H.Scott (renamed *Sandpiper*)
1954/60.	T.E.Harmer
1960/67.	A.J.Taunton
1967/70.	M.N.&P.A.Taunton
1970.	A.J.Taunton

39 *Widgeon* 1937. Designer & builder: W.F.Jermy. LOA. 22′
Owners:
1937/46.	W.F.&W.J.Jermy
1946.	P.P.Andrews
1947/52..	P.P.Andrews & J.O.M.Wedderburn. MC.
1952/84.	F.J.Waters
1984/88.	C.Gooch
1988/96.	M.C.J.&R.C.Sadler
1996.	Museum of the Broads

40 *Decoy* 1937. Designer & builder: H.T.Percival. LOA. 22′
Owners:
1937/46.	John C.Curl
1946/57.	John L.Abbott
1957/63.	C.&H. Bradshaw
1963/69.	J.Robertson
1969/72.	D.H.Blackburne
1972/86.	C.P.Scott
1986.	C.J.H.Scott & Mrs.M.J.Jordan

41 *Didler* 1937. Designer & builder: Richard Harmer. LOA. 22′
Owners:
1937/46.	R.D.H.Harmer
1946/7.	J.Dawson Paul
1947/65.	J.Stoveld
1965/85.	Mrs. F.J.C.Thwaites
1985/88.	Broads Authority
1988/90.	Rev.N.Khambatta
1990/96.	Museum of The Broads
1996.	R.C.&M.C.J.Sadler
1997.	H.Ferrier

42 *Lady Pamela* 1938. Designer & builder: Frank Beeching. LOA. 22′
Owners:
1938.	W.G.Jones & F.Beeching
1946/62.	W. Arnott Fowler
1962/67.	C.Gregory
1967.	P.Stannard

1969 - left as wreck at Barton Turf. 1972, "rescued" by Andrew Anderson (Hon.Treasurer) and used as playground for Thomas & Edward.

43 *Curlew* 1939. Previous names: *Bloater, Dark Lady* Designer & builder: Herbert Woods. LOA. 22'
Owners:
1939.   H.G.Woods (*Bloater*)
1939/48.   E.J.A. Chamberlin (renamed *Dark Lady*)
1948/53.   E.P.,T.J.& Miss D.E.Whelpton (renamed *Curlew*)
1953/58.   T.J.Whelpton & Mrs. L.J.Eastwood
1958/63.   Miss E.Eastwood
1963/65.   J.Russell
1965/69.   George Ebbage
1969.   A.J. Taunton
1969/76.   M.R.&A.S.Owen
1976/85.   Ian S.Miller
1985.   S.F.Read & T.Jacob

44 *Kipper* 1939. Designer & builder: Herbert Woods. LOA.22'
Owners:
1939/46.   W.G.Jones & Frank Beeching
1946.   Capt. Rushden R.N.
1947/48.   J.R.D.James
1948/58.   L.J.&Miss Eileen Eastwood
1958/66.   D.Rowley
1966.   T.H.Clarke

45 *Limelight* 1939. Previous names: *Whimbrel, Limelight*. Designer & builder: Herbert Woods. LOA. 22'
Owners:
1939/58.   H.G.Woods & D.Brock
1958.   Dr. G.Bolt
1958/62.   K.H.Flatman
1962/3.   N.Smith
1963/74.   F.C.&J.C.Clarke
1974/78.   D.Hogarth & Miss J.Clarke (renamed *Whimbrel*)
1978/83.   K.Bull
1983/85.   H.Platt
1985/89.   D.Saunders & J.Findlay
1989/00.   J.Findlay
2000/2.   T.Cave
2002.   G.Tibbenham

46 *Martin* 1947. Designer: Herbert Woods. Builder: Martham Boat Building Co., Martham. LOA. 22'
Owners:
1947/55.   Dr .& Mrs. B.M.Tracey
1955/63.   Dr .& Mrs. J.A.Eddy
1963/72.   H.A.O.Hartop & B.T.Keeble
1972/5.   K.G.R.Steggles
1975/7.   S.F.Read
1977/01.   S.J.P.Cooper
2001.   P.Bown

47 *Scoter* 1953. Designer & builder: Wyche & Coppock. LOA. 22'
Owners:
1953.   Norfolk Punt Club
1953/63.   Justin Scott

1963/65.	A.W.Faulkner
1965/68.	R.R.& H.M.Dowling
1968/87.	Capt.&Mrs.A.J.R.Tyrell
1987.	Dr. & Mrs. J.S.L.Fowler

48 *Melanitta* 1954. Designer & builder: Wyche & Coppock. LOA. 22′
Owners:

1954/62.	Dr. & Mrs. B.M.Tracey
1962/66.	A.W.Anderson
1966/70.	J.H.Nicholson
1970/79.	Mrs. V.A.T.Nicholson
1979.	P.Tracey

49 *Snark* 1957. Previous names: *Snark, Teal*. Designer: Wyche & Coppock. Builder: E.C.Landamore. LOA. 22′
Owners:

1957/66.	G.K.Snow & C.K.Arnold
1966/70.	C.B.Arnold
1970/78.	G.E.Daniels
1978/82.	J.L.Parker (renamed *Teal*)
1982/94	J.Forster
1994.	Rev. & Mrs. N.Khambatta (renamed *Snark* and extensively rebuilt)

50 *Greylag* 1958. previous name: *Flamer* Designer: Wyche & Coppock. Builder: Tom Harmer. LOA.22′
Owners:

1958.	Keith Flatman & Tom Harmer
1959/64.	T.E.Harmer
1964.	W.A.K.Edmunds
1965/67.	T.Ward (renamed *Greylag*)
1967/79.	David Adler
1979.	A.Southall
2005.	R.Parker

Flamer was the first Norfolk Punt constructed with built-in buoyancy.

51 *Harnser* 1961. Designer: Wyche & Coppock. Builder: Eastwood Whelpton. LOA. 22′
Owners:

1961/63.	Mr. & Mrs. J.M.Plaice
1963/66.	R.M.Huggins
1966/67.	R.McD.Cobb
1967/74.	M.T.Osborne
1974/03.	K.&T.A.Clarence Smith
2003.	J.Jarvey

52 *Wild Duck* 1961. Designer: Wyche & Coppock. Builder: Eastwood Whelpton. LOA. 22′
Owners:

1961/3.	W.B. de Quincey, G.T.Willis & Dr. D.Vaughan
1963/78.	W. B. de Quincey
1978/82.	P. Curl & J.Hoseason
1982/86.	Mr. & Mrs. J.W.N.Hoseason
1986/88.	J.C.W.Hoseason
1988/93.	D.Horne
1993/96.	R.Yaxley
1996/03.	R.Powell

2003.   D.Long

53 *Wild Goose* 1962. Designer: Wyche & Coppock. Builder: Eastwood Whelpton. LOA. 22'
Owners:
1962/9.   Dr. & Mrs. B.M.Tracey
1969/75.   Dr.B.M.Tracey
1975/79.   Dr. R.U.Carr
1979/83.   N.Monk
1983/02.   John Parker
2002.   J.Parker & J.Pye

54 *Tern* 1963. Designer: Wyche & Coppock. Builder: Eastwood Whelpton. LOA. 22'
Owners:
1963/73.   Dr.&Mrs.J.A.Eddy
1974/77.   Dr. J.A.Eddy
1977/79.   Dr.C.Skipper
1979/86.   S.Jenner
1986/92.   D.Wilton
1992/93.   R.Parker
1993/03.   J.M.Friend
2003.   J.M.Friend & S.Girling
2005.   Simon Jenner

55 *Kingfisher* 1963. Designer: Wyche & Coppock. Builder: Tom Harmer. LOA. 22'
Owners:
1963/97.   T.E.Harmer
1997/99.   J.Grime
1999.   R.Parker
2001.   Andrew Bell, Kim Whittaker & D.Baulcombe

56 *Puffin* 1966. Designer: Wyche & Coppock. Builder: T.E.Carter   LOA. 22'
Owners:
1969.   Mr.&Mrs.T.E.Carter
1976.   Old hull destroyed and replacement built by T.E.Carter
1982.   T.E.& Miss J.Carter

57 *Avocet* 1970. Designer: Wyche & Coppock. Builder: J.H.Scott. LOA. 22'
Owners:
1970/91.   J.H.&T.R.Scott
1991.   Mrs. C.R.&T.R.Scott

58 *Willow* 1972. Previous names: *Anas Acuta, Willow*. Designer: Wyche & Coppock. Builder: T.E.Ward. LOA.22'
Owners:
1972/74.   T.E.Ward
1974/78.   M.J.Lamb
1978/80.   Robert Green (renamed *Anas Acuta*)
1980/84.   Dr. & Mrs. D.J.F.Luckhurst (renamed *Willow*)
1984/01.   M.R.Q.Luckhurst
2001.   D.Long

59 *Firefly* 1972. Previous name: *Flounder* Designer: Wyche & Coppock. Builder: J.V.de B.Grey. LOA. 22'
Owners:

1972/75.	J.V.de B.Grey (emigrated to New Zealand)
1975/82.	K.G.R.Steggles
1982/87.	Robert Snelling (renamed *Firefly*)
1987/88.	R.Snelling & R.Parker
1989/91.	Roger Taylor
1991/94.	C.Jarvis & J.Clarke
1994/98.	R.Wilson & J.Symonds
1998/01.	D.Houghton & J.Symonds
2001.	C.Abel & R. Stephenson

60 *Lady Sylvia* 1972. Designer: Wyche & Coppock. Builder: J.E.Mockett. LOA. 22'
Owners:

1972/90.	J.E.Mockett
1990/99.	M.Sawyer
1999.	C.Williams

61 *Shoveller* 1975. Designer: Wyche & Coppock. Builder: Derek Gibbs. LOA. 22'
Owners:

1975/88.	D.Gibbs
1988/92.	Dr. & Mrs. J.S.L.Fowler
1992/99.	K.Roll
1999.	P.Wren & R. Slatter

62 *Hobby* 1976. Designer: Wyche & Coppock. Builder: R.McDonald Cobb. LOA. 22'
Owners:

1976.	R.McD.Cobb

63 *Bittern* 1976. Designer: Wyche & Coppock. Builder: J.V. de B. Grey. LOA. 22'
Owners:

1976.	J.V.de B.Grey

Built in New Zealand.

64 *Garganey* 1977. Previous name: *Golden Jubilee*. Designer: Wyche & Coppock. Builder: C.R.D.McDougall (GRP) LOA. 22'
Owners:

1977/79.	Fibreglass Norfolk Punt Fund Association
1979/86.	J.Parker
1986/88.	D.Horn
1988.	M.Thwaites & D.Potter
1989/91.	J.Riviere & C.H.Cator (renamed *Garganey*)
1991.	J.Pallister

Mould taken from 61 *Shoveller.*

65 *Reed Bunting* 1978. Designer: Wyche & Coppock. Builder (in plywood): S.F.Read. LOA. 22'
Owners:

1978/81.	S.F.Read
1981/88.	R.C.&P.J.K.Sadler
1988/02.	Dr.&Mrs.D.Roberts
2002.	Mac. Powell

66 *Grebe* 1978. Designer: Wyche & Coppock. Builder: Colin McDougall. (GRP) LOA. 22'
Owners:
1978.   G.A.Dunthorne
1985/88   R.Parker
1988/89.   C.W.Stewart
1989.   J.Parker
1989.   C.McDougall
1991.   Dr.&Mrs.R.Farman
200   Dr.P.Butters

67 *Swallowtail* 1977. Designer: Wyche & Coppock. Builder: Colin McDougall (GRP) LOA. 22'
Owners:
1977/82.   Colin McDougall
1982/85.   John Parker
1985.   A.George
1985.   A.George
1986.   M.J.Lamb
Swallowtail has the original GRP hull that the Fibreglass Norfolk Punt Association rejected as over weight.

68 *Ogo (Swordfish)* 1978. Design: Wyche & Coppock. Builder: J.V. de B.Grey. (Ply) LOA.22'
Owners:
1978.   J.V. de B.Grey
                 Built in New Zealand.

69 *Marsh Harrier* 1978. Designer: Wyche & Coppock. Builder: Colin McDougall (GRP) LOA. 22'
Owners:
1978/85.   C.Chapman & Miss F.M.G.Anderson
1985/94.   C.Chapman
1994.   Mr.& Mrs.& Miss C. Moule

70 *Barnacle Goose* 1980. Designer: Wyche & Coppock. Builder: Colin McDougall (GRP) Decked by S.F.Read. LOA. 22'
Owners:
1980/01.   D.H.Adler
2001   P.Adler
The first composite punt.

71 *Swift* 1980. Builder: Not applicable.
Owners:
1980.   S.J.P.Cooper
The registration fee only was paid for this punt, which was never built.

72 *Dipper.* 1981. Designer: Wyche & Coppock. Builder: Colin McDougall. LOA. 22'
Owners:
1981   J.D.Sennitt

73 *Razorbill.* 1985. Previous name: *Reedham Nan.* Designer: Andrew Wolstenholme. Builder: Fred Saunders. LOA. 22'
Owners:
1985/87.   John Findlay
1987/92.   J.C.W.Hoseason (renamed *Razorbill*)
1992/96.   J.Clarke

1996/05.   Neal Duffield
2005.   James Hoseason
Double chine prototype. Stitch and glue construction.

74 *Blackbird.* 1988. Designer: Phil Morrison. Builder: S.Read. (cold moulded) LOA. 22′
Owners:
1988/97.   R.C.&P.J.K.Sadler
1997.   C.Pilling
2005.   Simon Girling and John Friend

75 *Rainbow Trout.* 1989. Designer: Wyche & Coppock. Builder: (GRP) LOA. 22′
Owners:
1989/90.   M.Thwaites & N.Potter
1990/00.   M.& Miss L.Virden
2000.   J.&R.Rosser
2005.   Terry Vincent

76 *Kookaburra.* 1989. Designer: Wyche & Coppock. Builder: M.Hardy (GRP) LOA. 22′
Owners:
1989/95   M.Hardy
1995/00.   Mr. & Mrs.T.R.Lake
2000.   C.Bunn

77 *Rhode Island Red.* 1989. Designer: P.Morrison. Builder: Matthew Thwaites. (Foam sandwich hull, wooden deck.) LOA. 22′
Owners:
1989/92.   M.Thwaites
1992/3.   P.Carrington
1993.   Richard Parker
1993.   S.Wright

78 *Firebird.* 1990. Designer: Wyche & Coppock. Builder: Richard Parker. LOA. 22′
Owners:
1990.   R.Parker
Scrapped 1991

79 *Hushwing.* 1990. Designer: P.Morrison. Builder: Matthew Thwaites. (GRP/Foam sandwich) LOA. 22′
Owners:
1990/92.   W.Riviere & C.Cator
1992.   W.&T.Riviere

80 *Dabchick.* 1991. Designer: Wyche & Coppock. Builder: Colin McDougall (GRP) LOA. 22′
Owners:
1991/01.   Mr.&Mrs.W.I.Rhodes
2001.   J.Richards & F.Trappes Lomax

81 *Grayling.* 1991. Designer: Wyche & Coppock. Builder: Colin McDougall (GRP) LOA. 22′
Owners:
1994.   Mr.&Mrs. C.McDougall
2004.   Paul Watson

82 *Merlin*. 1991. Designer: P.Morrison. Builder: Richard Parker. (GRP. Foam/Kevlar/Carbon. Ply deck) LOA. 22'

Owners:

1991	R.Parker
1992.	D. & A.Wilton

83 *Honey Buzzard* 1991. Designer: P.Morrison. Builder: T.Hubbard(GRP/ply composite) LOA. 22'

Owners:

1994/97.	T.Hubbard
1999/99.	P.Shipley
1999.	K.Roll

84 *Swift* 1991. Designer: P.Morrison (modified) Builder: Matthew Thwaites. LOA:20'6"

Owners:

1991.	M.Thwaites
1992.	P.Carrington
1993	R.Parker

85 *Scoot* 1991. Designed & built by Fabian Bush, Rowhedge, Essex. LOA. 20'

Owners:

1991.	Dr .& Mrs. J.S.L.Fowler

Clinker ply with gunter rig.

86 *Peregrine* 1993. Designer: P.Morrison. Builder: R.Parker. (cold moulded). LOA. 22'

Owners:

1993/97.	R.Parker & R.Snelling
1997/03.	C.Wood
2003.	S.Clayton & R.Mockridge

87 *Shag* 1993. Designer: P.Morrison. Builder: South River Marine, St.Olaves. (cold moulded). LOA. 22'

Owners:

1993.	James Gill

88 *Cormorant* 1993. Designer: P.Morrison. Builder: M.Morrison. (cold moulded). LOA. 22'

Owners:

1993/03.	M.Morrison
2003.	S.Girling & J.M.Friend

89 *Goosander* 1994. Designer & builder: Fabian Bush.(clinker ply). LOA. 20'

Owners:

1999/00.	Miss C.Barron & Dr.R.A.Bayles
2000/02.	C.Tovell & M.Bown
2002.	James Deveson

90 *Saker* 1995. Designer: Phil Morrison. Builder: M.Virden. (cold moulded) LOA. 22'

Owners:

1999	M.&T.Virden

91 *Cuckoo* 1995. Designer: Stephen Jones. Builder: Fabian Bush. (clinker ply). LOA. 20'

Owners:

1995/02.	P.R.A.Bainbridge
2002.	J.Sallis

92 *Flamingo* 1999. Designer: David Horne. LOA. 19'
Owners:
1999.   A.Tibbenham

93 *Hummingbird.* 2000. Designer: David Horne LOA. 19'
Owners:
2000.   D.Pike

94 *Whooper.* 2000. Designer: Stephen Jones. Builder: Richard Faulkner, Hamble. LOA. 22'
Owners:
2000.   P.R.A.Bainbridge

95 *White Eagle.* 2002. Designer: P.Morrison. Builder: Richard Parker. LOA. 22'
Owners:
2002.   D.H.Adler

96 *Snowgoose.* 2003. Designer: Wyche & Coppock. Builder: John Parker. Hull: Jeff Green. Decks: J.Jarvey.
LOA. 22'
Owners:
2003.   John Parker

97 *Great White.* 2003. Designer: P.Morrison. Builder: Richard Parker. LOA. 22'
Owners:
2003.   Richard Parker

98 *Redwing.* 2004. Designer: Wyche & Coppock. Builder: John Parker. Hull: Jeff Green. Decks: A.Thaine.
LOA. 22'
Owners:
2003.   Arthur Thaine

99 *Woodpecker.* 2004. Designer: Wyche & Coppock. Builder: John Parker. Hull: Jeff Green. Decks: J.Jarvey.
LOA. 22'
Owners:
2004.   Chris Woods

100 *Jackdaw.* 2005. Designer: P.Morrison. Builder: Richard Parker. LOA. 22'
Owners:
2005.   Mark Critchley

101 *Emperor Goose.* 2005. Designer: Wyche & Coppock. Builder: John Parker. Hull: Jeff Green. Decks: J.Jarvey.
LOA 22'
Owners:
2005.   John Parker